LEGISLATIVE HONORS

TO

The Memory of

PRESIDENT LINCOLN.

MESSAGE OF GOV. FENTON

TO THE LEGISLATURE, COMMUNICATING THE DEATH OF PRESIDENT LINCOLN.

Obsequies of President Lincoln in the Legislature.

PRINTED UNDER DIRECTION OF
J. B. CUSHMAN, Clerk of Assembly.

ALBANY:
WEED, PARSONS AND COMPANY, PRINTERS.
1865.

STATE OF NEW YORK.

In Assembly,
Albany, April 27, 1865.

Resolved, That the Clerk procure four thousand copies of the proceedings and remarks in the Assembly Chamber on the death of the late President of the United States, to be printed in pamphlet form, for use of the members, officers and reporters of the Assembly.

By order.

J. B. CUSHMAN,
Clerk.

Note.—Although the resolution directing the publication contemplates only the proceedings of the Assembly, for the purpose of preserving, in an enduring form, the entire *Legislative* action upon the occasion, the proceedings of the Senate relative thereto are also included in the same volume.

J. B. C.

LEGISLATIVE HONORS

TO THE

MEMORY OF PRESIDENT LINCOLN.

MESSAGE OF THE GOVERNOR.

IN ASSEMBLY,
Saturday, April 15, 1865.

The private secretary of His Excellency the Governor appeared in the Assembly chamber and presented a communication from His Excellency, in the words following, to wit:

EXECUTIVE DEPARTMENT,
ALBANY, April 15, 1865.

To the Legislature:

It becomes my painful duty to announce to the Legislature the death of ABRAHAM LINCOLN, President of the United States.

It is with emotions of profound sorrow that I make this announcement to your honorable body. Such an event is a national calamity, and under the circumstances now attending this bereavement, the nation weeps with heightened anguish. To be deprived of his wisdom, experience and counsel, at a time when most important to return us securely to national peace, fraternity and prosperity; at a time when the gigantic war which confronted him at the threshold of his administration is about drawing to a close, and a final deliverance obtained from our civil disturbances, for which we have sacrificed so much, is a calamity that will cause the deepest sadness and gloom to the millions of our land and to the friends of freedom throughout the world.

Thus, it is the third time in our history, the Republic is subjected to this trial, but it is hoped that our good cause and country, watered by a nation's tears and sanctified by its prayers, will pass in safety through the ordeal to a higher life and destiny.

I have also to communicate to you the sad intelligence that our noble Secretary of State, an honored and favored son of New York, WILLIAM H. SEWARD, was likewise the victim of the tragic plot of the assassins, and now lies in an unconscious condition. May God spare his life to the nation.

R. E. FENTON.

In connection therewith, Mr. VAN BUREN offered for the consideration of the House a resolution, in the words following, to wit:

Resolved (if the Senate concur), That the message of His Excellency the Governor, communicating intelligence of the foul murder of the President of the United States and the attempted assassination of the Secretary and Assistant Secretary of State, be referred to a joint committee to consist of five members of the Senate and seven of the Assembly, to take order thereon.

The rule being suspended by unanimous consent, Mr. SPEAKER put the question whether the House would agree to said resolution, and it was determined in the affirmative.

Ordered, That the clerk deliver said resolution to the Senate, and request their concurrence therein.

A message from the Senate was received and read, requesting the concurrence of the Assembly to a resolution, in the words following, to wit:

Resolved (if the Assembly concur), That the message of His Excellency the Governor be referred to a joint select committee of five from the Senate and seven from the Assembly, and that the Legislature take a recess until one o'clock P. M. of this day.

The rule being suspended by unanimous consent, Mr. WOOD moved to amend said resolution by striking out the words "one o'clock P. M.," and inserting in lieu thereof the words "eleven and one-half o'clock A. M."

Mr. SPEAKER put the question whether the House would agree to said amendment, and it was determined in the affirmative.

Mr. SPEAKER then put the question whether the House would agree to said resolution, as amended, and it was determined in the affirmative.

Said resolution was then sent to the Senate, and was returned by that body with a message informing of concurrence in the amendment of the Assembly thereto.

In pursuance of said resolution, Mr. SPEAKER appointed as such committee, on the part of the Assembly, Messrs. VAN BUREN, WOOD, GLEASON, J. L. PARKER, REDINGTON, WEED and M'CONVILL.

At 10 o'clock and 50 minutes, the House took a recess until 11½ o'clock A. M.

At 11½ o'clock A. M. the Assembly again met, when, on motion of Mr. INGRAHAM, it was

Resolved, That the Superintendent of the Capitol is hereby directed to drape the Assembly chamber in mourning, and that the chamber remain so draped for thirty days.

A message from the Senate was received and read, in the words following, to wit:

" *To the Senate:*

"The joint committee of the two Houses on the message of his Excellency the Governor, this day transmitted to the Legislature, makes the following report:

" The committee having in mind that the funeral

ceremonies of the late President of the United States will probably take place on some early day in the next week, and that such day will be observed throughout the whole country as a day of solemn recognition of the tragic and awful event which now fills all thoughts, and that the Legislature will join in that observance, do unanimously recommend that on the day which shall be appointed for such obsequies, the two Houses of the Legislature do meet in their respective chambers at the hour appointed for such funeral ceremonies, and that the two Houses being opened with prayer, by clergymen especially selected for that service, resolutions appropriate to the occasion be offered; that the joint committee of the two Houses be now empowered to sit again to draft such resolutions, and to report them on that day to the respective Houses, and do report the following resolution:

"*Resolved* (if the Assembly concur), That the Legislature, viewing this unexampled and solemn event as demanding a cessation of legislative business, do now adjourn until Tuesday of next week, at 11 o'clock A. M.

CHARLES J. FOLGER,
Chairman Senate Com.
THOS. B. VAN BUREN,
Chairman Assembly Com."

By unanimous consent the rule was suspended, and the resolution unanimously adopted; whereupon, Mr. SPEAKER declared the House adjourned.

WEDNESDAY, April 19, 1865.
REV. DR. HALLEY'S PRAYER.

Almighty God, Thine is the power, the kingdom, the excellency; Thy works are perfect, and Thy ways are judgment. Heaven is Thy throne and the earth is Thy footstool; all nature is Thy temple and all space Thine abode. Deeply, O God! impress our minds with that great National bereavement that has spread such profound gloom over this people. We rejoice that there is nothing accidental or contingent in Thy procedure. How miserable should we be if we lived in a world which no Divine Wisdom presides to touch its springs and control its movement! But Thy word sweeps away the nonentity of chance, and teaches us that Thou reignest—that Thy providence embraces the vast and the minute, the remote and the near, regulates every law and guides every operation of nature—that the leaves of every flower are opened by Thee, that the particles of every dew-drop are collected by

MEMORY OF PRESIDENT LINCOLN. 9

Thee, that every volcano is convulsed and every planet is wheeled by Thee—that every action and volition of Thy intelligent creatures, whether so great as to affect the welfare of nations, or so minute as to flutter only for a moment in our atmosphere, is under the care of that Being for whose inspection nothing is too minute, and for whose power nothing is too vast. Almighty Father, how consolatory thus to believe, under the bereavements of life, that life is not a scene of trembling accidents, and that we do not wander along its paths with no hand to guide, no heart to sympathize and no voice to soothe us. "We will therefore lift up our eyes to the hills from whence cometh our help; our safety cometh from the Lord, who made heaven and earth." Nor need we wonder, great God, if Thy procedure should often be wrapped in deepest mystery to us. How can we, with our puny minds, scan the counsels and unravel the procedure of Thy infinite wisdom. Can man by searching find out God? If our children do not always understand the counsels of their parents, if our servants cannot fathom the plans of their masters, is it wonderful that in Thy procedure, whose dwelling place is eternity, whose duration is eternity, there should be heights we cannot reach, and depths vain for us to explore, crooked things we cannot make straight, and rough places we cannot make plain? We will, therefore, meekly bow when we cannot comprehend, and look forward to the sunlight of eternity, where all darkness shall be dispelled, and the connection between the sufferings of this life and the glory to be revealed shall be disclosed.

How consolatory, O God, are these views of Thy character to us under that solemn dispensation, that has struck like an ice-bolt on the heart of this country. Thou hast removed, by death, our worthy and beloved President. Thou hast called him from his post when his agency seemed necessary for carrying out those profound measures of his policy for the interests of our country. Thou hast caused him to be struck down in the vigor of his manhood and the meridian of his usefulness, in a manner harrowing to our feelings, by the pistol of the ruthless assassin. Almighty God, under such a calamity we will be still and know that thou art God. We will reverently bow to Him who has smitten us. We thank Thee for all that thou didst honor him as the instrument of doing for us. We thank Thee for his distinguished elevation, as an illustration, that in our country, nothing is insurmountable to talent and industry and integrity, and that these can enable its possessor to rise above obscurity of station, and occupy the most responsible positions. We thank Thee that, called in an important crisis to guide the destinies of his country, he displayed such wisdom and sagacity as inspired with confidence the hearts of his countrymen in that important struggle on which they were entering. We thank Thee for the firmness and energy of purpose he always displayed, so that in the blackest hour of his country's peril he guided the helm with a faith that never wavered and a hope that never sank. We thank Thee for that spotless integrity, that transparency of character, that guileless spirit he ever displayed, leading even those who censured his measures, never to suspect the honesty of his purpose. We thank Thee for those brilliant events that transpired during his administration—the triumph of law and order and constitutional government over treason and despotism, and furnishing deeds of patriotism and valor to which history affords no parallel. We thank Thee for that manly piety which he displayed, in his stated periods of daily devotion, his attendance on the sanctuary, and that marked recognition of Thy providence and sovereignty, which appeared in all his proclamations. And now, blessed God, Thou hast mysteriously taken him away. We bow to Thy wisdom. His body is now being conveyed to the congregation of the dead amid the throbbing hearts and streaming eyes of a people who feel each as deeply as if they had experienced a family bereavement. "It is the Lord, let Him do what seemeth good in his sight."

In the benevolent spirit of our holy religion, which enjoins us "to weep with those that weep," we commend to Thy paternal sympathy his bereaved partner and children. Do Thou, the God of the widow and the Father of the fatherless, sustain them in this hour of their desolation. Is there any sorrow Thou canst not assuage? any sorrow, the poignancy of which Thou canst not remove? any darkness, which Thou canst not dispel by a ray sent down from thine eternal throne? Comfort them in their mourning, and may they feel that whatever may befall them, they will ever be the subjects of cherished solicitude to the people. And do Thou bless our Secretary of State and his kindred, who were sufferers in the late awful calamity. We rejoice to hear encouraging tidings of their recovery. Do Thou raise them from the bed of sickness, and spare him, the intimate associate and counselor of the late President, that he may yet devote the energies of his enlightened mind to the interests of his country. And we commend to Thy protection and counsel him on whom, by death of our President, the onerous and responsible duties of Chief Magistrate now devolve. Clothed as he now is with the prerogatives of office, may he be endowed with all the necessary graces and qualifications for it; may he receive from Thee the wisdom profitable to direct, and may he surround himself with wise and enlightened counselors, who shall aid him in guiding his country through its present interesting crisis and carrying it to prosperity and glory.

Bless, O God, our land, the scene within these few years of such monstrous events. We thank Thee for our brilliant successes, by land and by sea, for the skill and energy imparted to our commanders and officers, and for the heroism and patriotism of our soldiers and sailors. Bring the murderous war, if it be Thy will, to a speedy close, stay the future effusion of blood, and may those insurgent States who have entailed such calamities on themselves and others, see the folly and wickedness of their conduct, and again live under the shades of the same paternal Government. And gratify our statesmen, who are soon to be employed on delicate and embarrassing questions, touching sectional interests and institutions, to adopt every conciliatory course connected with the rights of humanity to bring the disaffected back to the sway of our Government, and may the insurgents speedily return to loyal subjection, and thus peace and prosperity be enjoyed throughout all our borders.

Bless all the States of our Union in all their interests, agricultural, commercial, literary and religious; increase our schools and colleges, that the influence of a sound education may be enjoyed by our youth in fitting them for stations of usefulness and trust. May the sanctuaries of Zion be everywhere attended, and the elements of a sound and practical theology be taught from their pulpits; give our judges justice, and our executive righteousness, and may the gigantic war that is drawing to a close, teach us more than ever the importance of national individuality, and thus passing through this fiery tribulation, may we come out, renovated, regenerated, living in peace, studying to promote each other's interests, and may our land in the future enjoy a brightness that no cloud shall obscure, and a serenity that no storm of civil dissensions shall ever disturb.

Bless the State, its Governor; may he be eminently qualified for every duty devolving on him. We commend to Thee this House of Legislation. May every member bring to the discharge of his duties, an integrity of mind, a conscientiousness of purpose, and may all their deliberations be conducted for the advancement of Thy name and the interest of their constituents.

And now, Almighty God, impress on us the lessons of this hour. May the death of our beloved President not only affect our hearts, but lead us to reflect and act. Let us be preparing for death as an event certain in its occurrence and momentous in its results. Let us identify the duties and events of life with the retributions of a coming eternity. Let us believe the doctrines, obey the precepts, and be living under the hopes of religion. Then death will be the gateway of a blessed existence, and we shall close our eyes on earth to witness the shining shore and tread the golden streets of the New Jerusalem, and dwell eternally with God. AMEN.

Mr. VAN BUREN, from the joint select committee, appointed on the 15th, reported the following resolutions:

Resolved (if the Senate concur), 1st. That the Legislature of New York has received the announcement of the death of ABRAHAM LINCOLN, late President of the United States, with the emotions of profound sorrow.

2d. That in the character of the illustrious dead, were united the patriot and statesman, whose purity of purpose and wisdom of counsel have guided our Republic safely in its hour of greatest trial, and enshrined him in the affection of the American people.

3d. That this sad and afflicting event is a national bereavement, the more to be deplored, that his administration having well nigh suppressed the gigantic rebellion in the South, promised, as its crowning act of glory, the speedy and happy pacification of the whole country.

4th. That the unparalleled crime by which the nation has been deprived of the services of the chief of its own free choice, while in the active discharge of his duties, is not only revolting to the general sense of mankind, but is an outrage upon popular government, particularly deserving the execration of the American people, and consigning to eternal infamy its perpetrators and abettors.

5th. That we have the highest confidence in the patriotism, good sense, virtue and religion of the American people, and we believe, that even under this greatest of all calamities, they will exhibit to the world their regard for the Constitution and Laws of their country, their love of justice and order, and their firm reliance upon an all-wise and overruling Providence.

6th. That to God, who has been with this nation from the beginning, who, through the past four years of terrible war, has guided and protected us, and who of late, has so signally blessed us, do we turn in this day of our distress, and humbly commit ourselves and our interests.

7th. That while the country mourns its loss, its sympathies are due to the bereaved family of the deceased, and that His Excellency the Governor, be requested to transmit to them these resolutions, with the expression of the sincere condolence, in their great misfortune, of the people of this State.

8th. That to the Hon. WILLIAM H. SEWARD, Secretary of State, we tender our sympathy in his sufferings, and our hope for his speedy recovery, and we assure him that the murderous attempt to remove him from his sphere of usefulness, has only strengthened him in the love and confidence of his countrymen.

9th. That the Capitol be draped in mourning, and the members and officers of both Houses wear a uniform badge of sorrow for thirty days, and that it is recommended to all the citizens of this State to wear some symbol of mourning for a like period.

REMARKS OF MR. VAN BUREN.

MR. SPEAKER: I stand in the presence of this appalling calamity without language to express the emotions of my heart. We are living, sir, in the midst of startling and wonderful events. But yesterday, and the land was full of songs of rejoicing.

Every eye beamed with pleasure, and every voice was vocal with praise; when suddenly, while the skies were bright everywhere, while the sun was shining, while the birds were singing, and the flowers were budding—suddenly, while every heart was overflowing with joy, the lightning-flash was seen, the thunder-bolt rent the air, an earthquake shook the land, and dark clouds swept over the whole heavens. The electric message flashed throughout the Republic—

"THE PRESIDENT IS DEAD!"

The same foul spirit that has starved our prisoners of war in swamps and dungeons; that has tortured our wounded on the field of battle, and mutilated the bodies of our dead, has culminated in a crime so monstrous that history has no parallel.

Men looked at each other in dismay, and the nation staggered under the parricidal blow!

The chosen chief of the people, whose wise counsels and great heart have won him the confidence and esteem, not only, but the warm affection of his countrymen. He, who, representing a loyal nation, has, through four years of bloody strife, maintained its honor, established its power, and brought it to the threshold of Peace. HE, of all men, to die a death of violence, at the hands of a common cut-throat!

It is a fearful affliction, and more universal, even, than the *joy* over our national triumphs, is now the great *grief* over our loss. *Praise* has given place to *prayer — thanksgiving* to *lamentation*.

THE NATION WEEPS.

There is desolation in every home, sorrow in every heart. He was Chief Magistrate of the nation not only, but his kindness of heart, his earnestness of purpose, his purity of life, his pure, unselfish, devoted patriotism, has made him a place at every hearthstone in the land; and from every family altar his name has daily ascended to Heaven.

Sir, what is the meaning of this startling Providence?

I shall not undertake to interpret it, but I have confidence to believe that that Power which has sustained and blessed the nation thus far, will turn this dark affliction into a rich and permanent blessing.

In all our sorrow, we have not forgotten our duties.

THE NATION STILL LIVES,

The government still moves on — the people are still obedient to law, and no difficulty or danger is to be apprehended. Our wounded Secretary of State, saved as by a miracle, gives promise of returning health; our officers of government are spared to us, our generals are still in the field, our brave soldiers still stand the bulwark of the Republic. Our people, with one voice, gather around the new administration and bid it "God speed." The news from the national capital proclaims that he who now stands in the place of the illustrious dead, is worthy to wear his mantle. We have every reason to believe that the country will continue in its career of prosperity.

One thing, it appears to me, is already apparent in regard to the policy of the new administration; that, while the right hand of fellowship will, with returning peace, be held out to the misguided and misled people of the South, their leaders and betrayers, those foul spirits who have feasted upon treason, and cruelty, and murder, will be treated with proper severity. Let us, one and all, uphold the hands of our new President, and over the grave of the martyred dead, renew our vows to maintain the Union of our States, and secure the blessings of liberty to all who tread our soil.

Sir, the benediction is already upon us. In the wail of our common sorrow all party strife has disappeared, and I trust the future, that is to be born of this present, will be full of the fair fruits of this sorrowing communion.

Even now, sir, we can hear the rustling wings of the sweet angel of Peace. This earnest gathering speaks to us from the great heart of the people of a common country, of one glorious banner, of one blessed destiny.

The cold and stormy winter is melting into spring, and the warm and generous summer is hastening toward us. May we, sir, may the nation, realize the sacred assurance that "WEEPING MAY ENDURE FOR A NIGHT, BUT JOY COMETH IN THE MORNING."

REMARKS OF MR. WEAVER.

Mr. SPEAKER: For the first time in our national experience, resolutions like those under consideration, claim the attention of the American people. Suddenly and unexpectedly, we are summoned to pause in the presence of the most appalling event in our history. The President of the United States has been assassinated. A crime which has seldom been directed even against the instruments of despotic power, from which the oppressed had no means of relief, except by acts of violence, has at last been perpetrated upon our own elective Chief Magistrate. He who had passed unharmed through four years of civil war, during which those who inaugurated it doubtless imagined that they might succeed in overthrowing the government of which he was the head; he, against whom the bloody hand of the rebellion had not been raised when he was directing the energies of the country to its suppression, at last, after the dark night of our tribulation had passed, in the bright morning of the renewed existence of our government, has been stricken down.

Had the horrid deed been committed while yet treason claimed disputed sway over that portion of our domain which it attempted to appropriate to itself, and while it was directing its deadliest blows at every attribute of our government, though unapproached and unapproachable in infamy, it would have been surrounded by a becoming drapery of crime, in guilty harmony with its own abhorrent nature; but perpetrated as it was, in the early dawn of returning peace, in the first lull of subsiding conflict, and when the stern mandates of war were being tempered into generous invitations to a restored brotherhood, the victim falls like the tempest-beaten oak upon the highest mountain top, struck and shattered by a thunderbolt from a clear and tranquil sky, after the storm had passed. Separated completely from its relations to the government, and standing simply as the murder of ABRAHAM LINCOLN, a citizen, in times less fruitful in enormities it would have stirred the popular pulse, but when the blow is aimed, through the life of the President, at the government which he represented, all other crime pales to innocence in comparison; for when the assassin slew the President, he invaded the home of every citizen, and attempted to slay the first born principle of American liberty—the will of the majority, which, under our political system, is the constructive will of all.

From whatever source the crime originated, from whatever motives it was committed, it is an unmixed calamity to every section and to every interest of the entire nation. The shock itself is a calamity; the example is a reproach and a calamity; but the consequences will be most prejudicial to those who most need executive clemency.

At this hour the remains of an American citizen lie in state at the national capital. The mind that recently animated that form now prostrate in death, rescuing itself by its own native strength and vigor from the relationships of its early and humble career, won for its possessor promotion to the highest civil and political position in the land. Not yet commissioned to the place, every citizen had a right to dispute his claim; once lawfully licensed to the office, no man had a right by violence to disturb him.

This is not the time nor the occasion to discuss his

conduct, nor to sit in judgment on his particular acts. Whatever diversity of opinion there may have been in regard to the policy he pursued, all will concede to his character an element of simplicity, sincerity and earnestness, guided by vigorous common sense and animated by a disposition to do what he believed to be right. If his judgment was at times in error, if his selection of means was not always the wisest and the best, the embarrassing circumstances under which he was called into service, will go far to extenuate his faults and to propitiate the verdict of posterity.

The magnanimity of his conduct during the last few days of his life, toward the subdued people of the South, contains a strong appeal for a charitable construction of the earlier and severer measures of his administration, and is calculated to relieve the original doubts of many in regard to the motives that induced him to the exercise of unusual powers, and to vindicate the integrity of his purposes.

The calm bearing with which the nation has received this shocking calamity, and the composure with which the highest executive powers and responsibilities have been transferred from the lamented President to his constitutional successor, cannot fail to command the profound respect of the civilized world, and to inspire new confidence at home and abroad, in the stability of our institutions. An event which would have tended to produce division and disorder in other countries, has only served to draw this people more closely together, to renew a common vow that our government, having passed through the severest ordeal, shall, with the continued favor of Heaven, survive the attacks of its enemies, and live on to bless succeeding generations.

REMARKS OF MR. REDINGTON.

Mr. SPEAKER: I need offer no apology for occupying a portion of the time of the House on this mournful and melancholy occasion. The lights and shadows of life were never more forcibly illustrated, on the one side, than in the recent victories that crowned our arms, causing joy to thrill every patriotic heart, and opening up to our immediate view the termination of the war, resulting in an honorable peace; and on the other, in that tragic event that has deprived the nation of its President, clothed the land and inhabitants thereof in mourning, and stricken the heart of the people with grief. But little more than a week since, upon the reception of the news of our victories in this Assembly chamber, such was our delight, our ecstacy, our gratitude, that in the exuberance of the moment we lost regard for parliamentary decorum, and spontaneously burst forth in acclamations of unbounded joy.

But now, alas, how sad the change. We are here assembled in this chamber, draped in the sombre hues of lamentation, with hearts broken with grief, and shedding unavailing tears over the grave of the Nation's Chief.

This Assembly has often, heretofore, witnessed discussions that called forth a divided sentiment, and often an embittered feeling, but we are here now, sons of one common country, and lovers of one common flag, with our heads bowed to the earth like the bulrush, and covered, as it were, with sackcloth and ashes, to weep bitter tears over the untimely fate, the assassination of ABRAHAM LINCOLN, President of the United States.

We are all ready to exclaim from the broken fountains of our grief, O, that such a foul blot had never disgraced the American name; O, that such a wretch, capable of performing such an appalling act of wickedness, could ever have been born under the protection of the American flag!

History will do justice to the memory of ABRAHAM LINCOLN. Called to preside over the destinies of the nation at a period when its existence was imperiled by open and violent acts of treason, he had, with an honest desire to do right, carried us nearly through the most formidable civil war that history has ever recorded. Many of the measures that he had adopted for the suppression of the bloody contest, had, in some instances, as it was to be expected, passed through the ordeal of severe criticism ; yet the period of time had arrived, just previous to the fatal moment that so unexpectedly terminated his life, when a discerning public began fully to appreciate the patriotism of his designs, the honesty of his purpose and the magnanimity of his heart.

Nearly the last act of his life, notwithstanding all the provocations that would naturally lead to a contrary result, was meditating acts of mercy and forgiveness to those who had plunged the land in blood and draped it in mourning. His magnanimous heart was contriving some means by which the angel of mercy could arrest the hand of avenging justice. In the exercise of these thoughts he was rapidly gathering around him the sympathies of a large proportion of those who had thought it wise to oppose his administration. How this matter would have finally terminated, God only knows. At this important crisis in the history of our beloved country, when all eyes were fastened upon him with the most intense interest and anxiety, and the pulse of the nation was throbbing to its inmost centre—when fond hopes, as we thought, were soon to be consummated, and an honorable peace spread its balmy wings over a desolated land—it was then, *even then*, that a miserable wretch, a fiend in human form, had singled out his unsuspecting victim, and the President of the United States, by the pistol-shot of an assassin, is laid in the cold embrace of death.

Well may we mingle our tears together on this sad occasion, and weep with those that weep, and mourn with those that mourn. Well may we adopt the expressive language of Washington Irving: "O the grave! the grave! It buries every error, covers every defect, extinguishes every resentment; from its peaceful bosom spring none but fond regrets and tender recollections. Who can look down even upon the grave of an enemy and not feel a compunctuous throb that he should ever have warred with the poor handful of earth that lies mouldering before him?"

Allow me to add still further. How mournfully are we taught by this awful dispensation, that in the midst of life we are in death. At one moment the sun may shine down upon us in its meridian splendor, our pathway may be strewed with flowers, a kind

Providence may be conferring upon us unnumbered blessings; health, the choicest of heaven's blessings, may flush our cheeks; no disturbing hand to molest our peace or mar our social enjoyment. But soon! Ah, how soon, is this scene often changed, the sun suddenly hiding itself in darkness; over our heads gathers a cloud of impending storm, and out of that cloud comes down upon us a whirlwind of fury that scatters to the four winds every present or anticipated enjoyment, and lays our lifeless form with the dead. Such to us as individuals, are the changing scenes of human life.

It therefore becomes us as men, as legislators, so to live, in an uncertain life like this, "that if our earthly house of this tabernacle were dissolved, we have a building of God, a house not made with hands, eternal in the heavens." As God deals with us as individuals, so he deals with us as a nation. We may not be able to fathom the mystery that breaks in upon us so suddenly and with such terrific power; we may not be able to discover why it is that the head of the nation has, in this appalling manner, been summoned from his earthly labors—why it is that he has performed his last service and exercised his last thought in behalf of his bleeding and lacerated country. But what is incomprehensible to us is fully known to Him who ruleth nations; and the time will come, I think, when even to our limited vision, what is now incomprehensible, will be made fully to appear. All these things being so, let us never forget that we have inherited a government that will and must exist, whether in the sunshine or the storm, whether in adversity or prosperity, and that government having been established by the Almighty, will never fail, being properly maintained and supported by ourselves, to receive His constant care, the aid of His everlasting arm.

REMARKS OF MR. CUTTING.

Mr. SPEAKER: Did I consult my own inclinations, I should remain silent in the face of the appalling calamity which, in the inscrutable orderings of an All Wise Providence, has been visited upon the American people. Words, however sincere or eloquent, are wholly inadequate to express what every one of us so deeply feels, and the silent communing with our own hearts would best enable us to read, as we ought, the great lesson which is now so solemnly taught us. But in taking such humble part as I may in the sad ceremonial to which this day has been consecrated, I would join with the members of this House, and with good men everywhere, in expressions of respect for the memory of the lamented dead, of horror and detestation of the treason which led to his untimely taking off, and of regret that it has not been given to man adequately to punish the perpetration of so monstrous a crime.

A few days since, sir, and the people of this nation were exultant with hope. The long, dreary years of a desolating war were drawing to a close, and from amidst protracted scenes of darkness and of blood, beamed forth, at last, the light of returning peace. But in an instant, as it were, all this was changed. The blow of an assassin has turned our anticipated feasting and rejoicing into sadness, and in the moment of victory we are called to mourn a loss, the magnitude of which we are hardly yet prepared to appreciate.

Under any circumstances, the sudden removal of the head of a powerful nation, must be a great public misfortune; but in our circumstances it is a national calamity beyond the power of language to describe. For this reason we deeply and sincerely lament the death of our Chief Magistrate. But this is not all. The late President possessed a character peculiarly his own; and however men might differ in regard to the propriety of his political course, or the soundness of his policy, few would venture to deny to him the possession of qualities well adapted to win popular favor. He was emphatically a man of the people. And when political excitements had died away with the occasions which gave rise to them, and party asperities had been softened by the influence of great events, the people honored and respected him while living, and they sincerely mourn for him now that he is dead.

"Peace hath her victories, no less renowned than war."

And such a victory, in the midst of arms, had Mr. LINCOLN achieved over that portion of the people, who, from their honest convictions, had not yielded to all the measures of his administration their cordial support. While conquering old prejudices, he built up in their hearts new hopes of a bright and better future. His ardent desire for a restoration of the old fraternal feeling among the people of the States, as manifested in the last acts of his administration, and his kind, conciliatory and humane policy toward repentant rebels, with a view to this great result, had demonstrated to men of all parties, the kindliness of his nature and the purity and disinterestedness of his patriotism. Had he lived, sir, to carry out this policy, he would have united as one man in its support, the great mass of the American people. And, because he did not live to consummate the last and most glorious act in the great national drama, the whole country is clothed in mourning, and a great nation awaits in silence and in tears, the passing by of the last sad procession. As is known to this House, I am not of those who contributed to elevate the late President to his great office; but in the light of recent events I had come to regard him as one in whom were centered, in great measure, the destinies of the Republic. His death, with its awful circumstances, shocked me no less than it shocked every one of us here. I grieved for a good man fallen, and trembled for the future. But, sir, a part of that future has already come. The President is dead, but the nation still lives; and in the sublime spectacle afforded by the peaceful passing of our government from the dead to the living, we have an earnest that all will yet be well. It rests with others to finish what was so well begun. If they are faithful to the people, the people will be true and faithful to them. History will record the virtues of ABRAHAM LINCOLN, and a restored Union and a reunited people will be for him a monument more enduring than brass or marble, more precious than silver or gold.

REMARKS OF MR. J. L. PARKER.

Truly, Mr. SPEAKER, a great man has fallen, and the people mourn. Just as the angel of peace spread her white wings over the land, covering a country the future greatness of which no mortal can foresee, and a people re-united, having one common purpose, one hope, one nationality and one destiny, and just as the joyous refrain was pealing forth from every belfry in the loyal States, and the whole country had been lit up with bonfires and was resounding with hosannas for that coming peace, the President of the United States, who had contributed more than any one man toward crushing out this foul and unhallowed rebellion, and to whom the people were, as one man, looking for a fair, impartial and honorable settlement of the difficulties by which we were surrounded, was stricken down by the hand of an assassin, and our rejoicing is turned into sorrow, and our hosannas into lamentations.

As a nation, we are to-day standing at the feet of death, and gazing with tearful eyes into the grave where our hopes are sought to be buried. Of Mr. LINCOLN's character nothing need be said. He needs no eulogium. His record is made up, written in characters of living light. His great energy, his patience in adversity, his honesty of heart and his sublime perseverance, are all matters of record, and as such are interwoven with the history of the country; and in after times when history and tradition repeat by the side of every fireside in the land the story of the hardships and the sufferings of each of the heroes of this war, it will be said of ABRAHAM LINCOLN that he, too, never faltered. With a sublime determination to wipe from our national honor the foul cause of the rebellion, he was always consistent. Manly and modest in character, forgiving and generous to a fault, his memory will grow greener and sweeter in the hearts of his countrymen with every returning year. Faithful and consecrated to the service of his country, he pressed on to the accomplishment of its salvation, regardless alike of the howling of enemies and the complaints of pretended friends. As the star in the east guided the wise men of Herod over the hills and through the valleys of Judea, even unto the cradle of a Saviour, so has ABRAHAM LINCOLN been to his people the star in the east, guiding them over the hills and through the bloody valleys of this rebellion, even unto the cradle of a blessed, and, as we fondly hope, a lasting peace.

There exists not in the recorded deeds of the great names of the dead past, nor yet among those of the living present, in all the nations of the earth, a grander, more glorious, a greater or nobler record than that of ABRAHAM LINCOLN; and the coming millions who are to people this vast country will honor and revere his manly virtues and his exalted patriotism, as we to-day honor and revere the virtues and self-sacrificing patriotism of our loved and immortal WASHINGTON.

REMARKS OF MR. ANGEL.

Mr. SPEAKER: In view of the sad and melancholy circumstances by which we are surrounded, and of the solemn services in which we are engaged, I have persuaded myself to attempt to give some feeble expression to the feelings and emotions with which every heart seems to be filled at the awful calamity that has befallen our nation and people.

It is not simply the head of the nation that has been stricken down by the assassin's arm. A great, and wise, and good man has been taken from us — one whom we trusted and had learned to love, and each and every one of us feels the sad bereavement as he would the untimely loss of a member of his own immediate household.

The highest eulogy of ABRAHAM LINCOLN is found in the universal gloom and sorrow that pervades the land, and the emblems of mourning that meet the eye on every side speak more eloquently than any words the deep and all-pervading grief of every member of the community. It was a great achievement, in the wild and stormy times that have attended his administration of the government from its very commencement, to have secured the respect and confidence of every party and all classes of the people. It was a prouder triumph still, to have won his way to the admiration of the world, and the approval of all good and just men throughout the universe, under difficulties and trials and temptations that have seldom or never beset the ruler of any people. Still nobler and more enduring is the monument he has erected in the hearts of millions of his fellow men — the poor, the humble and the helpless, whose lot it is to toil, endure and suffer, and who never yet have failed to find in him a wise, considerate friend, and a sincere and conscientious champion of their rights. By these he will be mourned and cherished while memory lasts, and those who come after them for many generations, will bless the name of our martyr President, and feel that they are better and happier men for the recollection and contemplation of his virtues and example.

I do not propose on this occasion to indulge in eulogy or biography. The historian will do ample justice hereafter to one of the most remarkable men of this or any age, and to his treatment of the greatest and most desperate revolutionary movement to overturn a good and beneficent government the world has ever witnessed. In the struggle now about to close, he had overcome the arms of the enemies of the republic, and was fast effecting a conquest of their hearts. If anything more than another exhibits the intense and malignant wickedness of the rebellion, it is the fact that it raised its treacherous arm against the President's life, when his heart was filled with forgiveness, with the words of pardon on his lips. It would almost seem as though Providence had inclined the actors in this bloody tragedy, with their own parricidal hands to close the door of mercy, and thus leave justice alone to execute its office. Like the hate that rejected the Saviour of mankind and nailed Him to the cross, the spirit of the rebellion scoffed at proffered pardon, and in its blindness struck down the hand that would have rescued them from the penalties of perjury and treason.

It is fortunate for the credit of our race, that the world can furnish so few examples of such atrocious wickedness, and in our dealing with this instance of monstrous depravity and crime, may we not expect that the result will be a terrible warning to evil doers in the time to come, against any attempt at its repetition?

But, sir, I do not propose to speculate on the results likely to follow the great crime we are considering. At the present moment we can only contemplate the loss we have sustained, and mingle our sympathies with those who have been so sadly bereaved. Next to the family of our lamented President, the nation has most occasion to grieve. At a great crisis in our history — at a moment when wisdom, prudence, firmness, and a wise consideration of public measures was requisite to secure and establish peace on a basis that could never hereafter be disturbed, the arm on which we leaned has been taken from us, and the great heart that throbbed with love for those who had so deeply offended, and would have saved them from the consequences of their madness and delusion, has gone down to its rest in the slumbers of the grave.

God help those for whom he prayed and labored, for they will have need of kindly offices in the sore tribulation yet in store for offenses such as theirs.

In adopting the resolutions presented by the committee of this Legislature, we are but doing justice to ourselves, and rendering the tribute due from the great State of New York to one she loved and honored while he lived, and whose memory she will cherish, and whose virtues she will emulate, now that he is gone.

But, sir, it is gratifying to feel, that under the sorrow that has bowed us down, there is hope and brightness in the future. We are assured that the sun is still shining above the clouds that are hovering over us, and that ere long the light of peace and prosperity in all its fullness will again be ours. Never before was our government as strong as now, when, after an occurrence that would have convulsed other nations, and overturned thrones and dynasties, we stand unmoved, save by the great grief that fills our hearts; and the functions of government in any of its departments have not been disturbed for a single hour. With entire confidence in him who succeeds our noble and lamented chief, with confidence in the affection of the people for the institutions under which we live, we have little cause for apprehension or for mourning, save over the grave that is about to close upon the remains of one we had learned to love so well. In a nation's tears he receives a tribute to his goodness and worth that is accorded to few, and we all know and feel that not only ourselves, but the country and the world at large, are wiser and better for his having lived and labored here. In his great and good example — in the purity of his life and the integrity of his purpose — he has left to us a legacy beyond all price, and takes his place in the records of our history by the side of those sages and heroes whose memory we delight to honor, and of whose immortality we hope to partake.

REMARKS OF MR. GLEASON.

ABRAHAM LINCOLN is no more!

We gather with sorrowing hearts and weeping eyes to pay the last sad tribute of respect to his memory. His career of strange vicissitudes is ended, and "after life's fitful fever he sleeps well." Shall we mourn for him?

> "We tell thy doom without a sigh,
> For thou art Freedom's now, and Fame's;
> One of the few — the immortal names —
> That were not born to die."

His sun goes down in full-orbed splendor, without a cloud to mar its beauty. His honors culminated at the very period when death snatched him away, and he has left but little behind that he could have desired to gain. From obscurity he had come to be the head of a mighty nation. He had again been chosen to fill that station. He had labored through long and weary and gloomy years, through evil and through good report, to crush the power of the rebellion, and the end drew near. Just when all hearts were turned toward him more than ever before, just when he seemed about to be the President, in fact, of the United States, just then his summons comes, and his spirit flies to the God who gave it.

How near he was to us we never knew till we lost him. We were used to smile at his homely ways, but the great, noble, generous heart beneath, and his keen, vigorous intellect, had won our love and our respect, so that a general grief falls upon all. Witness for him, ye weeping mothers, who to-day fill our land with sorrow and mourning, because he is not. Witness for him, ye strong men, bowed in agony of heart, and sighing away the still hours of the night. Witness for him, ye marts of commerce and of gain, now dumb and forsaken. Witness for him, ye scarred veterans of the battle-field, who have so often faced death at the mouth of the murderous cannon, and who have seen without a murmur your bravest and your best stricken down. Now, all unmanned, you pour out your grief, which cannot be suppressed. Witness for him those whom he led out of the house of bondage, and to whom his name is hallowed as their deliverer. Witness for him the friends of freedom, the downtrodden and the oppressed in all lands, who have followed his course with earnest wishes and with prayers, and to whom he has been as "the shadow of a great rock in a weary land."

Gone is now all censure and rebuke. Gone is all partisan approval and all partisan reproach. His failings and his faults lie buried in his grave and shall there be forgotten, while his good deeds shall alone remain, and alone be remembered. Over his sea of life swept many a turbulent storm, but around the little green mound that marks his resting-place those storms subside, and all is peace. The time, the place, the occasion, impress us with their solemnity, and call us to reverent hearts and to better lives. Before us opens the grave of our murdered President. About us stand the weeping, distracted millions of our countrymen. Far away float the dim clouds of war and rebellion. Above us God sits, who doeth all things well. Oh, my friends, let us heed the lesson this event brings home to us, and thus may we turn even this bitter cup to our own good and the welfare of our beloved land. Let it not be the fleeting impulse of the moment, but the solemn, determined purpose of our lives. From his grave there comes to us a voice. It bids us forget our selfish aims, old jealousies and party hates, and consecrate ourselves renewedly and entirely to our country and to mankind. It bids us know the full value of our Union, which has cost so many lives, but never a more precious one than this. It points us to his pure and upright life, his simple ways, his homely wisdom, his unwavering patriotism, his devotion to the public good. It urges us to prove ourselves worthy of the heritage for which he gave himself, and to stand in our appointed place firm and unyielding, till our end, too, shall come.

A new star shines to-day in our firmament. A new hero is enshrined in the temple of liberty. A new martyr is offered upon the altar of freedom. The lifeless form of our President is given to the tomb, "earth to earth, dust to dust, ashes to ashes," there to repose till the last angel bid the dead awake; but in the hearts of millions shall his memory endure till time shall be no more.

> There is no death! The stars go down
> To rise upon some fairer shore;
> And bright in Heaven's jeweled crown
> They shine forevermore.
>
> There is no death! An angel form
> Walks o'er the earth with silent tread,
> He bears our best loved things away,
> And then we call them "dead."
>
> Born into that undying life,
> They leave us but to come again;
> With joy we welcome them — the same,
> Except in sin and pain.
>
> And ever near us, though unseen,
> The dear immortal spirits tread;
> For all the boundless Universe
> Is life — there are no dead.

History has recorded in letters of living light the names of those in all ages, of whom the world was not worthy, who were caught up from loathsome dungeons, from torturing racks, from blazing piles, from the scaffold and the gibbet, to undying fame. She has taught us, by glorious deeds and glorious examples, that many have dared to die for humanity, and in that death have found immortality. She has made mankind nobler by such examples of heroism. But scan her pages as we may, search all ancient and all modern lore, read with tear-dimmed eyes the epitaphs of the good and the great of dead generaations, yet shall the name of our martyred hero glow as brightly, and his deeds be recorded as proudly as any of that long procession who have gone before.

America, fruitful of heroes, gives another to their company. Thank God for such a country!

Thank God for such a man!

REMARKS OF MR. PITTS.

When a good man dies the Nation mourns. Doubtless I express what others feel in common with me, when I say that this is one of the saddest days of my life. From my youth I have been taught that my country was to be preferred before my own kindred — before parents, or wife or child. When a blow is struck which robs us of the Chief Magistrate of the nation, that blow robs me also of my best friend. We can hardly yet realize the loss we have suffered, it came so suddenly upon us. A few days since, the booming of cannon, the rejoicings of the people, were heard everywhere throughout the loyal North, and flags and banners and illuminations were everywhere seen. We had reached a time when we saw just before us, and ready for us to enjoy, the fruits of our labors, the termination of the struggle, the prospect of an enduring and honorable peace.

The time had come when the array of hostile armies was to give place to the councils of peaceful political life; when the wisdom, statesmanship and sagacity of our Chief Magistrate, which had guided us so successfully in the stormy scenes of war, was to aid in restoring harmony and unity to our land. With faithfulness and skill, with a self-sacrificing devotion and Christian patriotism, that has never been excelled, he was engaged in gathering up and uniting in one, the separated strands of our national destiny, when the sad event we deplore occurred. Just as the dove returned to the ark of our national safety, bearing the tidings that it had found a place where to rest its foot, the cruel blow of the assassin took the life of the man in whom was centered the hopes of the American people. This is indeed to us a strange, a mysterious, a mournful occurrence. What a spectacle do we this day present to the civilized world! But not to dwell upon this, I remark, that we have here a lesson presented to us that we may do well to learn, and that gives us hope and trust. We see that this government of ours, no matter what wicked schemes may be brought to assail it, will live and is destined to endure throughout all time. We see that He whose power controls and shapes our destiny, will not permit that any designing arts or any shock of treason, shall prevail against us. For four years we have known the vicissitudes of war. The shadow of death has been cast upon every threshold, and every hearthstone has its vacant place; but the greatest loss of all is the loss we now deplore. No other sadness has been like that we feel, as we contemplate the fact that the grave is soon to receive the mortal remains of our loved and honored President. But in this as in all our losses, we learn the lesson of the stability of our government. Though our arms had met with reverses; though our flag had been trailed in the dust; though our pride had been humbled upon the seas, we were finally victorious. Just as peace was dawning upon our land, he who has guided us through many troubles has been stricken down, yet our country still lives, and days of promise and bright prospects are before us.

To-day the American people pause in their career, and stand with bowed heads around the grave of ABRAHAM LINCOLN. Let us forget all our political differences and animosities; let us resolve that henceforth and forever nothing shall divide us, and that this country and its government shall be preserved for all time — come what will, cost what it may. What other lesson than the stability of our government is here taught none may tell. If it be the will of the Disposer of all events to teach us by this sad calamity that magistrates are ministers of justice to execute his vengeance upon traitors, may this lesson be made so plain to us that a wayfaring man need not err in reading it.

ABRAHAM LINCOLN was a man above partisan strife, and who lived for his country; who knew not fear; who was "serene amidst alarms;" who was strong in faith and "invincible in arms." I believe that the union of these States was the great, grand object of his life; and it was his highest wish that this government should continue and be perpetuated through all time. With such objects and motives, what one, more than he, deserves our praise? In the circle of fame, there is a single summit that rises above all others and pierces the heavens. On that summit there are places for two only.

WASHINGTON, who prayed to the God of battles, who won for us our liberty, who gave to us our Republic, occupies one of those places; ABRAHAM LINCOLN, who, through the past four years of conflict and of strife, has by his patriotism, his energy, his wisdom and perseverance, rescued our Republic from traitors, has gained for himself a niche in the temple of Fame, and takes his place by the side of

the Father of his country, the immortal GEORGE
WASHINGTON. To-day is a time of special grief and
mourning, and my heart feels sad as I now remember that State which in the years of this conflict has
lost two illustrious citizens — the State of LINCOLN
and DOUGLAS. To-day they sleep their last sleep;
they have both fallen. Taking different views of the
political questions which agitated their country, they
may yet both be regarded as martyrs in this great
contest, as truly such as the soldiers who have
fallen in the charges or assaults made at Petersburg
and Richmond. Some future Homer will sing the
praises of those brave men who have thus fallen.

ABRAHAM LINCOLN is no more; but his life and
his example may still teach us lessons of virtue and
of wisdom. I beseech you and all loyal men, as you
have regard for the memory of the patriots, to listen to
the voice which comes from his grave. It urges that
we shall carry out the policy which he had begun, that
we shall firmly stand by and support his successor
and the government. Slaughtered by the deadly
bullet of an assassin, in the prime of manhood, it devolves upon others to carry forward the work which
he thus suddenly left unfinished and incomplete.

God will, I believe, protect us and make our cause
prosper. The bright day of peace will, I trust, soon

be ushered in, and events which to us seem dark and mysterious may be made to minister to this end. There is not a mother in the land but wets her pillow with tears as she prays that the death of our President may tend to harmony and peace. Gray-haired sires, as they wring their hands in sorrow for our bereavement, beseech God to give peace to our distracted country, and have hope as they recognize in this calamity the hand of Him "who doeth all things well." In the course of human events these clouds will pass away; the sun will shine again, and joy and happiness will return. This great country, cradled between two oceans, will be worthy of him who has been its President, and will be the freest, happiest, and proudest nation on the face of the earth.

REMARKS OF MR. RIDGWAY.

I feel profoundly impressed with the saddening and terrible event, which convenes us here to-day, and in uttering these sentiments, Mr. Speaker, I am sure I do but echo the sorrow which wells up from the hearts of every class of individuals throughout the wide extent of our country. Party politics are for a time hushed. A pall hangs over the nation, for we are called upon to mourn the sudden death, and by violence, of ABRAHAM LINcoln, President of the United States. He died when he could least be spared. He died when he was most beloved by the American people. Through his forbearance and magnanimity toward the chief soldier of the rebellion and his immediate army, he induced them to lay down their arms; and thus, within the last fortnight of his life, he inaugurated peace for this torn and suffering land, and caused joy and rejoicing to ascend from every hearthstone. It was at such a time as that, Mr. Speaker, when, as I said before, he was most beloved, that like another great ruler, Henry the Fourth, of France, he was stricken down by an assassin's hand, and has left a nation to mourn his untimely end. It is, therefore, meet and proper, Mr. Speaker, that this representative body should testify in a becoming manner the bereavement we all so deeply feel in the death of the Chief Magistrate of the nation.

REMARKS OF MR. WILBER.

Mr. Speaker: By reason of sickness, I was not present at the meeting of this body yesterday, when I had supposed that these words of remembrance and regret, for one who has fallen, would have been spoken. Unexpectedly I find myself to-day one of the mourners, as I may say, at the grave of the President. We are mourning for one, the loss of whom no poet can adequately sing, no pen or pencil adequately portray; no tongue can give utterance to that which we this day feel. Yet from the fullness of the heart, words find utterance, and hence I have asked the forbearance of the House for a moment. All of us would bow the knee in reverence, would express our heartfelt sadness, in regard to him whose loss we now deplore, in whom were centered, in a remarkable degree, goodness and greatness. It may be asked, then, why we should thus mourn, why we should thus express those feelings of sadness we share in common, one with another? It is fitting that we should thus lament when a great and good man dies. The ways of God are not our ways, and they are to us often mysterious. A day like this calls for trust in God, for faith in his overruling providence. God in his mercy permitted the foundations of this great nation to be laid; he favored us as a people, and led us on from small beginnings to unparalleled prosperity. Now, we may well ask why it is that he allows that a man, so good and so much needed as he who has been stricken down, should be taken from us? The Almighty Ruler alone knows why, and it becomes us to bow humbly to his dictates.

Our form of government has been regarded by other nations as an experiment. We have given proof in times of peace and of war, that if it has been an experiment, it was a successful one, and that our government possessed the element of stability. One test more was left for us — one further trial of the principles of free government. That test was, that the executive head of the government should be thus suddenly stricken down by his own child. I say his child, for the assassin was an American citizen, and we have called our Executive, FATHER ABRAHAM. I ask you, has there been a name more worthily given since the days of WASHINGTON? He was the father of the nation. In his bosom were feelings of kindness, even for the enemies of his country. Truly, he was FATHER ABRAHAM — he whose goodness had taught the world to respect him, whose kindness of heart and generous feelings, and whose mercy have been excelled by none upon earth, since the days when our blessed Saviour was among men in bodily form. During the four years of contest now drawing to a close, he was constantly harassed and knew no rest. Now, as brighter days were dawning for our country, as in this glad spring time nature was rejoicing, he was permitted relaxation.

He, with his family, took a single hour from the labors incident to his high office for enjoyment and repose. His iron visage, marked with the traces of the conflict through which he had passed, bore for the time the smile of merriment. It was just then, when the moment of relaxation had come, when the smile was upon his features, that the assassin took his life. That smile, as it were the smile of an angel, lingered upon his face in death. Thus the good man died; thus his spirit left us. He left his home on earth for a dwelling not made with hands, eternal in the heavens.

What a day of mourning is this! We have known days when other nations were in tears; but for us as a nation, the day of mourning has scarcely been known until now. The sad day has at length come to us also. When we received intelligence of our loss, on Saturday last, how the men of this House looked at each other. If every one had received intelligence of his own father's death, there could not have been greater sorrow. Not one of us had the heart to utter a word. Silent tears were streaming down manly cheeks. To-day we have scarce recovered from the shock, so profound was the grief of every heart; to-day we see on every hand the signs of mourning, the habiliments of woe. And this is because he whom we loved to call FATHER ABRAHAM is dead. ABRAHAM LINCOLN was both President and father of our country. He came from humble life, from the poor, and he knew how to remember them. The lowly and the oppressed, the widow and the orphan, and all of us in every part of this great land, both north and south, have cause to mourn as nation never mourned before.

We stand now by his grave; and where is that grave? It is in the heart of every loyal American. Soon his mortal remains will be borne from the capital of his country, and restored to his native State, to the home where he lived in private life, to which he has never returned since four years ago he went to Washington to assume the weighty responsibilities of his office. They will bury him there, and the blossoms of the fair West will grow and bloom from the soil that rests upon his bosom. The lovers of liberty will, by their praise of his many virtues, erect the best monument to his memory.

REMARKS OF MR. SHEPARD.

Mr. SPEAKER: I am sorry that ABRAHAM LINCOLN is dead. Slavery *now* is also dead. The late President is one of the very few in all history who needs no monument. Already Slavery has reared a monument of human bones, surmounted by the skulls of captains and generals. As such, by the action of God's elements, in a short time it will dissolve into the deep forgetfulness of oblivion, whilst the memories of those who battled for the right will weave themselves into the sacred traditions of every loyal household in the land.

Mr. LINCOLN was not only the martyr of a great cause, but the victim of a generous belief in the gratitude of those whose past crimes had been forgiven. His heart asserted its supremacy over his intellect, and caused him to forget that the lowest crimes of the dark ages could be engrafted upon the refinements of a civilization just now glittering in the rays of the new morning light.

Confronting the proffered pardon, this fiend of Slavery disbands its armies and renews the contest by assassination. Let no pretexts or sophisms becloud the mind. It is true, Slavery is dead; but the malignant passions which belong to it survive, and find their expression in crimes which compel us to notice the enormity, and what was the educational tendency, of this great national sin.

The tornado of civil war, arising from opposing currents, in its course uprooting strong oaks and unroofing the hearthstones of sacred households, has swept over the land, leaving the calm sun to shine out again upon its rainbow which now spans the blood-sprinkled earth.

For over two centuries the streams heading at Plymouth Rock and Jamestown have been increasing in volume and slowly converging, until, in this death, they have united into one. Just now, as we emerge into the deeper and broader waters of the great stream of time, God, for some wise purpose, has changed the pilot of the ship of State.

May the new one be as discreet in his management of the ship as was the dead captain whose memory we so fondly cherish.

FRIDAY, April 21, 1865.

The Senate returned the concurrent resolutions relative to the death of ABRAHAM LINCOLN, late President of the United States, with a message that they had passed the same, without amendment.

Whereas, it is represented that the remains of the deceased President, ABRAHAM LINCOLN, will pass through the principal cities on the line of the Central railroad, and that a brief stop will be made in this city; therefore,

Resolved (if the Assembly concur), That a committee consisting of three from the Senate and five from the Assembly, be appointed to meet those having the remains of the deceased in charge, at the city of New York, and accompany them through the State; and that the Lieutenant-Governor be added to that committee as the chairman thereof.

The rule being suspended by unanimous consent, Mr. WOOD moved to amend said resolution as follows: Insert after the word "appointed," the words "to act in concert with the Governor of the State, and the commander of this division, deputed by the War Department for that purpose, and with the municipal authorities of Albany, in perfecting arrangements for the reception of the body of the deceased President at the Capitol of this State," and Mr. SPEAKER put the question whether the House would agree to said amendment, and it was determined in the affirmative.

Mr. SPEAKER then put the question whether the House would agree to said resolution, as amended, and it was determined in the affirmative.

SATURDAY, April 22, 1865.

Mr. PITTS offered for the consideration of the House a preamble and resolution, in the words following, to wit:

Whereas, the great calamity that has befallen the

country, whereby the people of this State should leave nothing undone to testify their love and solemn veneration for the heroic deeds and public services, reflecting lustre on the country at large, of the late President, ABRAHAM LINCOLN, whose untimely death we are called to mourn,

Resolved (if the Senate concur), That His Excellency Governor FENTON be hereby requested to invite the Hon. HAMILTON FISH, President of the State Society of the Cincinnati, and a committee of three of said society, to meet at the Capitol in the city of Albany, on the 25th day of April, 1865, at 10 o'clock A. M., to concert measures to accompany the remains of our late lamented President to Springfield, Ill.; and that His Excellency be hereby authorized and requested to make such suitable and proper arrangements as may be necessary for the occasion.

The rule being suspended by unanimous consent,

Mr. SPEAKER put the question whether the House would agree to said resolution, and it was determined in the affirmative.

Ordered, That the clerk deliver said resolution to the Senate, and request their concurrence therein.

PROCEEDINGS

IN THE SENATE.

SENATE PROCEEDINGS

ON THE

DEATH OF PRESIDENT LINCOLN.

MESSAGE OF THE GOVERNOR.

IN SENATE,
Saturday, April 15, 1865.

The private secretary of His Excellency the Governor appeared in the Senate chamber and presented a communication from His Excellency in the words following, to wit:

EXECUTIVE DEPARTMENT,
ALBANY, April 15, 1865.

To the Legislature:

It becomes my painful duty to announce to the Legislature the death of ABRAHAM LINCOLN, the President of the United States.

It is with emotions of profound sorrow that I make this announcement to your honorable body. Such an event is a national calamity; and under the circumstances now attending this bereavement, the nation weeps with heightened anguish. To be deprived of his wisdom, experience and counsel, at a time when most important to return us securely to national peace, fraternity and prosperity; at a time when the gigantic war which confronted him at the threshold of his administration is about drawing to a close, and a final deliverance obtained from our civil disturbances, for which we have sacrificed so much, is a calamity that will cause the deepest sadness and gloom to the millions of our land and to the friends of freedom throughout the world. Thus, it is the third time in our history, the Republic is subjected to this trial; but it is hoped that our good cause and country, watered by a nation's tears and sanctified by its prayers, will pass in safety through the ordeal to a higher life and destiny.

I have also to communicate to you the sad intelligence that our noble Secretary of State, an honored and favored son of New York, WILLIAM H. SEWARD, was likewise a victim of the tragic plot of the assassins, and now lies in an unconscious condition. May God spare his life to the nation.

R. E. FENTON.

Mr. FOLGER offered the following resolution:

Resolved (if the Assembly concur), That the message of His Excellency the Governor, be referred to a joint select committee of five from the Senate and seven from the Assembly, and that the Legislature take a recess until one o'clock P. M. of this day.

The resolution was unanimously adopted and transmitted to the Assembly, where it was amended by fixing the time of meeting at 11½ o'clock A. M., which was concurred in by the Senate.

The PRESIDENT appointed as such committee, on the part of the Senate, Messrs. FOLGER, MURPHY, ANDREWS, COOK and SHAFER.

11¼ O'CLOCK, A. M.

Mr. FOLGER, from the select committee, submitted the following report:

To the Senate:

The joint committee of the two Houses on the message of His Excellency the Governor, this day transmitted to the Legislature, makes the following report:

The committee, having in mind that the funeral ceremonies of the late President of the United States will probably take place on some early day in the next week, and that such day will be observed throughout the whole country as a day of solemn recognition of the tragic and awful event which now fills all thought, and that the Legislature will join in that observance, do unanimously recommend that on the day which shall be appointed for such obsequies, the two Houses of the Legislature do meet in their respective chambers at the hour appointed for such funeral ceremonies, and that then, the two Houses being opened with prayer by clergymen especially selected for that service, resolutions appropriate to the occasion be offered; that the joint committee of the two Houses be now empowered to sit again, to draft such resolutions, and report them on that day to the respective Houses, and do report the following resolution:

Resolved, By the Senate (if the Assembly concur), that the Legislature, viewing this unexampled and solemn event as demanding a cessation of legislative business, do now adjourn until Tuesday of next week, at 11 o'clock A. M.

CHARLES J. FOLGER,
Chairman Senate Com.
THOS. B. VAN BUREN,
Chairman Assembly Com.

The report of the committee was adopted by the Senate.

The Superintendent of the Capitol was directed to drape the Senate chamber in mourning on the day of the funeral.

The Assembly concurred with the Senate in adopting the report of the committee, and

The Senate adjourned.

WEDNESDAY, April 19, 1865.

REV. DR. SPRAGUE'S PRAYER.

Rev. Dr. SPRAGUE, of Albany, offered prayer, as follows:

Almighty and All Gracious God, we bow before Thee as the Sovereign and Lord of the creation; as the God of all the nations of the earth. Thou hast ever been the God of this nation, guiding us amidst dangers, guiding us through difficulties, and helping us in all our times of need. But we have been disobedient to Thy commandments and ungrateful for Thy mercies; and Thou hast, in righteous retribution, suffered a dark cloud to settle over our national prosperity—when we imagined ourselves secure, we awoke to the appalling discovery that we were in the midst of the horrors of a desolating war. And that war thou hast suffered to rage with fearful fury during four consecutive years. At length we thought the cloud was beginning to move—we recognized, in a succession of glorious victories, the welcome harbinger of a better day. But just at the moment when our hearts were beating high with joy, because the bow appeared in the cloud, Thou hast commissioned a barbed arrow to strike the heart of the whole nation—he whom the nation had chosen to be its head has been stricken down in a moment by the hand of an assassin. And this is the hour in which the nation is looking up to Thee, from the depths of funeral gloom, to ask that Thine all gracious and all sustaining arm may be revealed in this time of awful calamity.

And first of all we desire to commend to Thee those whose hearts are bleeding from a disruption of the tenderest ties of life: the widow, from whom Thou hast taken the husband of her youth; the children whom Thou hast bereaved of a devoted and beloved father; and all the other mourning relatives, we commend to the consolation of Heavenly grace. Wilt thou cheer them amidst all their desolation by the tokens of Thy love? Wilt Thou enable them to bow submissively before Thine hand, to trust Thee implicitly amidst all the darkness, and to lay the solemn event to heart, that it shall be greatly subservient to their preparation for a better world?

We commend to Thee our newly inducted President, upon whom has so suddenly devolved the mighty responsibility of superintending and directing the mechanism of our government. We implore for him the needed wisdom and grace and strength from on high. Wilt Thou save his life from becoming a sacrifice to incarnate fiends? Wilt Thou inspire him with that unwavering confidence in Thee that will make him strong and earnest in the discharge of his duty? Wilt Thou cause his administration, while he has yet only entered upon it, to be signalized by the restoration of peace, and, in its progress, may it scatter the richest blessings throughout the length and breadth of our land.

We commend to Thy special blessing the several members of the Cabinet over which the departed President has so long presided. While they are devoutly thankful that their lives have been preserved in the midst of such imminent peril, let them gird themselves for fresh devotion to the interests of their country. Let there be light and wisdom in their minds; let there be courage, and constancy, and faith, and hope in their hearts; and let all the measures they adopt, be such as will meet Thine approbation, and find a grateful response from every patriotic bosom. May the Secretary of State, who was also the object of a murderous attack, and his son and assistant, who was marked as another victim, be mercifully spared and restored to health and soundness; and may they bring away with them from the scene of their sufferings such a sense of obligation to God, and such impressions of duty to their fellow men, as shall render their lives the more valuable to their country for having been thus imperiled.

We commend to Thee all who hold offices of public trust, whether executive or legislative, throughout our land, and pray that this solemn dispensation may make them wiser and more useful in the exalted stations they occupy. We specially commend the Legislature of this State, and more especially the branch of it here convened. With this expression of their sorrow may there be joined a reverent and devout recognition of Thy providence, and may there come to each of them, through these solemn services, a fresh baptism, not only of enlightened patriotism, but of earnest thought, and of devout feeling. As their annual term of legislation is about to expire, may Thy gracious providence attend them to their several homes, and reunite them with whom they love in the enjoyment of the best of domestic blessings.

And now, Father, what remains but that we leave our bleeding country, with all its varied interests, in Thy gracious care. We look to Thee to repair the desolation; to restore to us peace; and to unite this great nation again in goodly coöperation for the benefit of the world. We thank Thee for all that our lamented President has done for us; and now that his work on earth is accomplished, we pray that we may help to perpetuate his usefulness by giving heed to the lessons which come to us from his grave. So teach us to number our days, in view of this most solemn dispensation, that we may apply our hearts unto wisdom. Let us account it a blessed privilege to live for our country, but let us see to it that we live also for God and for Heaven. And while we labor diligently to promote our country's welfare, let us realize that all the springs of our national safety and greatness are in Thee, and that without Thy guiding and sustaining and helping hand, our efforts will be utterly powerless.

And now wilt Thou graciously preside over the exercises of this House, and let all things be done to Thine acceptance and honor? We offer Thee our prayer, in the name of Jesus Christ, our Redeemer. AMEN.

Mr. FOLGER, chairman of the committee, offered for the consideration of the Senate the following resolutions:

Resolved, 1st. That the Legislature of the State of New York has received the announcement of the death of ABRAHAM LINCOLN, late President of the United States, with emotions of profound sorrow.

2d. That in the character of the illustrious dead were united the patriot and statesman, whose purity of purpose and wisdom of counsel, have guided our Republic safely in its hour of greatest trial, and enshrined him in the affections of the American people.

3d. That this sad and afflicting event is a national bereavement, the more to be deplored that his administration, having well-nigh suppressed the gigantic rebellion in the South, promised, as its crowning act of glory, the speedy and happy pacification of the whole country.

4th. That the unparalleled crime, by which the nation has been deprived of the services of the chief of its own free choice, while in the active discharge of his duties, is not only revolting to the general sense of mankind, but is an outrage upon popular government, particularly deserving of the execration of the American people, and consigning to eternal infamy its perpetrators and abettors.

5th. That we have the highest confidence in the patriotism, good sense, virtue and religion of the American people; and we believe that, even under this greatest of all calamities, they will exhibit to the world their regard for the Constitution and Laws of their country, their love of justice and order, and their firm reliance upon an all-wise and overruling Providence.

6th. That to God, who has been with this nation from the beginning, who, through the past four years of terrible war has guided and protected us, and who of late has so signally blessed us, do we turn in this our day of distress and humbly commit ourselves and our interests.

7th. That while the country mourns its loss, its sympathies are due to the bereaved family of the deceased, and that his Excellency the Governor be requested to transmit to them these resolutions, with the expression of the sincere condolence, in their great misfortune, of the people of this State.

8th. That to the Hon. WILLIAM H. SEWARD, Secretary of State, we tender our sympathy in his sufferings and our hope for his speedy recovery; and we assure him that the murderous attempt to remove him from his sphere of usefulness, has only strengthened him in the love and confidence of his countrymen.

9th. That the Capitol be draped in mourning, and the members and officers of both Houses wear a uniform badge of sorrow for thirty days, and that it is recommended to all the citizens of this State to wear some symbol of mourning for a like period.

REMARKS OF MR. FOLGER.

Mr. PRESIDENT: But that the proprieties of the occasion demand a few words upon the resolutions I have reported, as chairman of the select committee, I should have preferred to have been silent. For what can one utter, that is not already in the throbbing heart of the nation? What is the word of any one, but the fond, vain attempt to voice the dumb agony of this afflicted people? Who shall fitly speak for this stricken community? No one, save him who hath acquired the power, in the language of JOHN MILTON, "by devout prayer to that Eternal Spirit who can enrich with all utterance and knowledge, and sends out His seraphim, with the hallowed fire of His altar, to touch and purify the lips of whom He pleases."

Less than one short fortnight ago, the Chief Magistrate of this commonwealth, in accordance with the glad feelings of the whole community, made proclamation of a day of jubilee and thanksgiving, "for the bright prospects of returning peace and fraternal harmony." So man proposes. That day has not yet come. And here we sit, in the shadow of a great sorrow, amid the external drapings of mourning, and with a mighty grief grasping at our souls and stifling all our powers. For the Chief Magistrate of the greater commonwealth has fallen, done to death, by the foul blow of the assassin. So God disposes.

The loss, the calamity, is ours. His—the lamented ruler—his is the profit, the great gain. Other Presidents have died. But none when the tangled skein of vast and mighty and pregnant policy lay yet unraveled in their trusted fingers, and a hoping, longing people waited in patient, confiding reliance for the great result. Other leaders, other great men of the nation have died. But their memories needs must wait for the haze of years settling upon the horizon where their sun had set, to refract the rays of burning prejudice, and to mellow the heat and hate of partisan aspersion. No other President, no other leader, no other great man of the nation, save one, has passed away in blood, and that one, though he may not have sought, did not avoid the occasion. And the tragic interest which, surrounding the name of HAMILTON, draws to his memory the tearful sympathy and regard of succeeding generations of his countrymen, in an accumulated degree, will keep ever green in fond and passionate remembrance the idea of ABRAHAM LINCOLN. The act of the murderer was the apotheosis of the victim.

It is hardly possible for us, the men of his own time, busy with the practical issues which engrossed his own great soul—it is hardly possible for us to analyze, with entire correctness, all the elements of character which, in their subtle affinity, took such close, firm hold of the popular feeling, and made him the acknowledged, the holy-anointed leader of the people.

ANDREW JACKSON was an almost omnipotent leader. It was his imperious, overriding, to-nought-yielding will, wisely directed by the greatest natural sagacity, that enabled him, the "cloud-compelling Jove," to sway the masses to his purposes.

HENRY CLAY was a leader. The scope of his power had a limit, and reached not beyond the irresistible fascination of the happiest personal manners, and the seductive persuasion of the most graceful rhetoric and elocution.

DANIEL WEBSTER was a leader. There was an awe about him. It was as if one of the gods had come from out of the clouds about Olympus, and lighting upon a "heaven-kissing hill," stayed for mortals to render him his due reverence.

It needs not to lessen or to disparage these to lift up the departed President. He differed from them all. Lacking somewhat of what they had, he had somewhat of what they all lacked. And it was by this that he laid his hand upon the heart of the people, and it beat responsive to his touch. ABRAHAM LINCOLN—the wisest and oldest sage in the land veiled his wisdom before his heaven-flashed sagacity, and the most timid child looked into his loving eyes and instinctively sought a cradle in his bosom. The famed warrior of fierce and bloody battles recognized his moral courage and knew him as a hero; and the erring, the lawless, the condemned to death, blessed the kindly, yearning, loving nature that oft and oft again gave the life-saving pardon. Burdened with the cares of state, such as no one ever had laid on human shoulders, he crisped the surface of the deep current of grave affairs with the light zephyrs of a kindly hilarity, and solved perplexing problems of momentous politics with facetious explanations — parable illustrating precept. His head was sound and right. His heart was great, and good, and loyal—loyal to the people, whose servant he was; loyal to the law which he ministered; loyal to the great idea of the Republic which he magistered; loyal to the God who, ruling in the universe, set him to rule on earth, in part thereof. Chosen to his position of elective Chief Magistrate by a minority of the people, he had come to sit upon a throne of the hearts of all, and had so gained upon doubtful friends, and so won upon open enemies, as that no mortal name in all this fair land was, on the day of his violent death, more coupled with affection, with hope, with blessing, with aspiration, and with confidence, than his.

And yet he died, suddenly, by violence, in ripe manhood, on the top of Pisgah, looking to the goodly, peaceful Canaan toward which, for weary years, he had toilingly led his people.

As for him who has thus gone, in the power of his manhood, in the rich strength of his intellect, in the noontide of his glory, in the climax of his fame, ere old age had come upon him, when he should be,

"With withered fist, still striking at death's door:"

apart from an allowance for the natural longing for prolonged life; apart from the god-like desire to behold the progress of humanity, and to see the work of our own and of others' hands established, we must regard his life and death as fortunate. He and his administration will be, for future ages, a most luminous point in American history. And this last, sadly horrid act in his conspicuously eventful life, while it makes for his memory an endeared and affectionate remembrance in every American household, is at the same time the lens of fate, pouring upon his name and his character and career the concentrated rays of the light of time and the intensified effulgence of history.

He lived, and acted, and did, and *refrained to do*, that men might "learn more worthily to understand and appreciate what a glorious gift God bestows on a nation when He gives them a true, and wise, and just, and noble, and gentle ruler."

"In war was never lion raged more fierce;
In peace was never gentle lamb more mild."

He essayed no single great achievement which, while it dazzled, should confuse, but not too far in advance of the people, he did ever, not too soon, nor yet too late, guide them to the fitting climacteric of all the turmoil and confusion, and strife, and waste, and blood of this quadrature of years. "He was a rich storehouse for the glory of God and the relief of man's estate."

With all the war powers of the Constitution in his grasp, until his advent, hidden in their secret crypt, and enough, if selfishly used, to make him the most absolute ruler in the world, we see him yearning, striving for that prevailing peace which should, by its coming, remit those vast powers to their recess, reduce him, the Military Commander-in-chief, capable of illimitable space, to the simple Chief Magistrate, rounded by the narrow circle of fixed and written law. Here, truly, was a humble, but a god-like soul, for "by our spirits are we deified."

And now, "lingering on the spot where a spiritual hero has sealed his faith," what lesson is there for us who survive, and who stand in amazement almost stupid at the portentous event. The saying of EDMUND BURKE is recalled: "When bad men conspire, good men must associate." As LINCOLN and all his powers were consecrated to the country which he loved, and the people who loved him, so, in such degrees as we may be able to lash our laggard natures, let us be consecrated. Let us allay partisan strife; let us frown on greed for office, and that canker of our institutions—office sought and used to glut the greed for gain; let us be of parties only in the higher sense, in that sense in which they are necessary to the welfare of a free state, when men unite to forward great principles, which, rooted back in eternal laws, reach forward toward ages yet to come. Let us cultivate that nobler ambition, which, if it is conscious of high and splendid qualities, seeks place and power to be of use to the commonwealth, or if modestly claimant of good intentions only, will consent to wait and serve in any ever so humble position, so that public good is achieved and the best interests of universal man advanced.

REMARKS OF MR. MURPHY.

Mr. PRESIDENT AND SENATORS: No event has ever so shocked the sensibilities of the community as the tragical occurrence over which we are now assembled to mourn. The high position of the departed President, his kindly virtues, the manner of his death, and the circumstances of the country, have all combined to evoke an universal cry of lamentation and woe. Appalled in the face of the greatest calamity that could befall the nation, and, as if touched by one common chord of sympathy, the arm of industry is suddenly paralyzed, the marts of commerce are deserted, and courts and legislative assemblies suspend their deliberations. In this general demonstration of our loss there is no division, no sect, no party, among us. ABRAHAM LINCOLN belonged to the country; he was the constitutional head of the whole republic. And while you, who assisted in elevating him to his high office, pour forth your sorrow, we, who have no such relation, seeing in his violated person wounds inflicted on the Constitution, on the majesty of the people and on the American character, behold in him the martyr to freedom and good order, and with you approach the bier, which this day bears his lifeless form, to deck it with funereal wreaths, and to bedew it with our tears.

It adds doubly to the poignancy of the public grief that this misfortune deprives us of his services at a moment when all eyes and hearts were turned toward him with the highest hopes and expectations. The rebellion, which for years had been draining the blood and treasure of the nation, which had threatened its very existence, till good men were almost despairing, had been crushed; and he had intimated a policy toward the insurgents calculated to reunite the States in fraternal bonds as well as in political relations. The blessings of millions of people were pouring in upon him, when all of a sudden the cup of joy and gladness is turned into bitterness and sorrow. We have lost Presidents before while in office, but never has such a realizing sense of their loss been felt by the entire community.

It was in the relation which Mr. LINCOLN occupied to this civil war that his importance is seen. He was not, in the common acceptance of the term, a great man; but he became great in his mastery of the greatest subject which has ever engaged the attention of man. For four long and weary and bloody years, the responsibilities involving the perpetuity of this nation and the salvation of republican institutions upon the face of the globe, have rested upon his shoulders. Amid jarring opinions and interested advice and timid counsels and weak commanders, he has been compelled to guide the shattered ship of state through a civil war, unparalleled in its violence in the history of the world. He had become the depository of the plans and views of all the parties and interests in the country, and had opportunities to know, better than any other man, the temper of the people north and south. He could view the whole field, and he did it with the comprehensiveness of a statesman who disregards sectional feelings when they conflict with the paramount interests of the whole body of the people.

Mr. LINCOLN was conservative by nature and by position. I knew him as I know you, Senators, whom I have met in the performance of duties here, having served with him in the councils of the nation while he was in Congress. Genial and kind hearted, generous impulses were the law of his nature. I have never seen him since our official connection; but when a few months ago I took occasion to address him in behalf of a case of suffering humanity, I received a prompt and favorable reply, showing not only that neither time nor distance nor difference of political sentiment had affected past friendship, but that his severer duties to the country did not prevent him from considering the claims of individuals upon his merciful prerogative.

He has gone, however, from us forever, and his spirit is with the God who gave it. Let us improve the lesson of his loss by imitating his example of devotion to our common country. That country survives, with its varied interests and its greatness undiminished—the hope of mankind and the dread of despots only. It has undergone a trial which no popular government has ever passed through safely. Let us show ourselves in history the great exception. Military power must now yield to the civil authority, and law and order resume their wonted sway. The deflections from the proper order of things, consequent upon our internal disorders, forgotten, we may then say:

> Her heroes slain, awhile Columbia mourned;
> But, crowned with laurels, Liberty returned.

REMARKS OF MR. COOK.

Mr. PRESIDENT: A great and good man is dead. The people mourn. The chosen head of this great nation has been stricken down in the zenith of his usefulness, and this, too, at the very time when his greatness and goodness were being fully developed, in his, I think I can say, successful efforts to restore peace and consequent prosperity to our bleeding nation.

Not struck down by any of the usual agencies through which the dark angel of death seizes his victim, but by the hand of an assassin. Humanity shudders at the deed, and as the telegraph conveys the terrible catastrophe to the people, the national pulse ceases for a moment to beat. The fiendishness of fratricidal *Cain* stands eclipsed by the monstrosity of the act.

ABRAHAM LINCOLN, President of these United States, was assassinated at Ford's Theatre, in the city of Washington, on the evening of the 14th of this month, and the assassin leaps from the presence of his murdered victim upon the stage, shouting " *Sic semper tyrannis.*"

Thus, if it were possible to add additional horror to the scene in applying this motto to the dying President, he uttered a lie whose depth is so deep as to be unfathomable, whose width is so wide as to be immeasurable.

ABRAHAM LINCOLN a tyrant! Why, Mr. President, if he failed in his duty in any one particular, it was that during this terrible rebellion, which began at the moment he assumed the responsibility of Chief Magistrate of the United States, he tempered justice with too much mercy. Sir, there was hardly a day passed that we did not see in the public prints notices of commutation and pardons of the sentences of both civil and military courts, passed upon offenders against the majesty of the law.

There was one prominent trait in the character of

the late President that stood in front of all others. It was that goodness of heart, that kindness of spirit, toward the errors of humanity, that almost appeared to look upon crime as seen by other eyes, as an offense which need simply to be repented of to be forgiven.

I stand not here to eulogize the late President. Acts are enduring memorials of men, words are evanescent. But when the history of this bloody rebellion is truthfully written, the world will say that ABRAHAM LINCOLN'S name and fame shall stand side by side with that of WASHINGTON, the Father of his country, as the preserver and protector of the glorious inheritance bequeathed to this people by our forefathers. And like him, not stupendously great in any one characteristic quality, but with an intellectual power so well balanced for the position which he occupied, as to master and use to the best advantage for his bleeding country, every emergency that arose during this unhappy rebellion.

It is useless to speculate upon the motives that led the assassin to the commission of this deed, as well as to undertake to fathom the causes that led to the attempt upon the life of Mr. SEWARD, Secretary of State.

There appears but one possible reason for this double assassination, and in my opinion it was an

MEMORY OF PRESIDENT LINCOLN. 87

attempt to strike down the efficiency of the administration to reconstruct and unite the discordant elements, that are now almost destroying our unhappy country.

This double assassination, executed at the same time and at different localities (although we have hopes that the life of Secretary SEWARD may be saved and his usefulness unimpaired), stands before the world without a parallel or example in the annals of history.

We know that rulers of nations have been assassinated while at the very acme of their power. We also know that they were rulers by the so-called "divine right of kings," or by force of arms over their subjects.

They exercised individually supreme power over the life, liberty and happiness of their people, governed in their action toward them only by whim, caprice or prejudice. Under such a despotism, oppression may have become so unendurable and intolerable (as in the case of the reign of terror of Robespierre in France), that assassination might almost become justifiable, as the only way to rid the world of a monster in human form.

But that assassination should raise itself to a successful issue in a government like ours, where all rulers are chosen by the people themselves, with entire power to change those rulers when they become obnoxious to the governed, from any cause whatever, and that, too, at short and stated periods, is a fact that sets at defiance the teachings of experience, and, as I have before said, stands out beyond a parallel or an example.

It exhibits a depravity in human nature that must produce a degree of humiliation upon every mind, that an individual man can so pervert the ends and aims of his existence as to make him a fit companion for the father of all evil.

Mr. President, thank God that the foundations of our Republic are laid so strong and deep, by the wisdom of our forefathers, that they are beyond reach of the bowie knife or the pistol of the assassin. The government still "lives, moves and has a being." Neither are its powers or purposes changed by this sad event.

Although this terrible catastrophe has placed the supreme power of the nation in other hands than those of the lamented LINCOLN, who now receives this power is one, also, chosen by the people to meet precisely the present condition of the nation. I have entire faith that he who has now entered upon the arduous duties of Chief Magistrate of these United

States, guided by the experience shed upon his path by the acts of the late President and his advisers, with the assistance of that Providence which watches over the affairs of nations as well as men, will conduct our country to peace, and to that prosperity which always follows in her train.

Just four years ago the attempt was made to assassinate our nationality. That attempt has now finally culminated in the cold-blooded murder of the chosen chief of this nation; and to the long list of illustrious dead, who have laid their lives upon the altar of their country's liberties, is now to be added the name of the martyred ABRAHAM LINCOLN.

REMARKS OF MR. ANDREWS.

Mr. PRESIDENT: We stand beside an open grave, a grave yawning and importunate for all that remains of him who, a few hours ago, was the embodiment of much of the history and still more of the hopes of this nation. Humble in his origin, gentle in his nature, firm in his resolve, merciful in his disposition, placable in his temper, ABRAHAM LINCOLN had proved a wise, skillful and successful pilot through the terrible storm of passion and civil war, which, for four long years, had jeoparded the ship of state. At the moment when peace is descried; amid salutes and streaming banners and joyous acclamations, he is stricken by the fell hand of an assassin; and to-day funereal drapery, and lowered flags, and the measured, mournful cadence of ordnance attest, but, oh! how feebly! the grief of a whole people.

The remarkable self-control of Mr. LINCOLN was an element in his character which contributed largely to his success. The wisest of men has said that "He that is slow to anger is better than the mighty, and he that ruleth his spirit than he that taketh a city." The waves of faction and the tumult of civil war beat wildly and fiercely about him, yet his serenity was never disturbed. Anxiety might cloud his brow, doubt and apprehension oppress his heart, but his calm judgment and clear perceptions were never swayed or obscured. There was true greatness.

Upon the occurrence of sudden and great national calamities, man instinctively seizes the lamp of history and searches the dim aisles of the past to find a parallel or precedent, and then by the aid of his reflective faculties strive to throw that light into the dark vista of the future, that he may divine something of that which is reserved for him.

In 1584, another republic was smitten with a grief like ours. The Prince of Orange, the father of the

Dutch Republic, in the maturity of his years, in the hour when his country was emerging from civil strife, in the presence of his wife, was shot to death by an assassin. Of the condition of his country, and of the value of his life to her, we may judge when the historian declares that, while William lived, "notwithstanding the spirit of faction and the blight of a long civil war, there was at least one country, or the hope of a country, one strong heart, one guiding head, for the patriotic party throughout the land." These words might well have been said of him whom we lament to-day.

In many personal characteristics there was a marked resemblance between the great Prince and the great President. I may be pardoned for alluding to one. The historian tells us that, "in the darkest hours of his country's trial, he affected a serenity which he was far from feeling, so that his apparent gaiety, at momentous epochs, was even censured by dullards, who could not comprehend its philosophy, nor applaud the flippancy of William the Silent."

The Dutch Republic survived its mighty founder for two hundred years. Nor will this Republic fail or falter because of any man, however gifted or beloved. Our tearful eyes, looking beyond the narrow tomb of our dear President, see a resplendent future for our country, and we, with humble faith, exclaim, in the language of Israel's king, "God is in the midst of her, she shall not be moved; God shall help her and that right early."

REMARKS OF MR. WHITE.

Mr. PRESIDENT: Until the last breath leaves the last citizen of this republic, two days shall be vividly remembered — the day of unsuccessful liberticide, which began this rebellion; the day of too successful parricide which ended it.

But, between those two days, what a tremendous unfolding of history! Day and night, as from some mighty loom driven by divine forces, has come forth this wondrous web of events which we now see completed — its warp the thoughts and acts of statesmanship — its woof the thoughts and acts of generalship. And as it has steadily rolled forth, like "some storied tapestry" from "looms of Arras or Cambray," it has revealed, day by day, week by week, wrought into its texture, such scenes as the world never dreamed. There stand deeds of patriotism, and deeds of rebellion; devoted acts, and intriguing acts. One week and it is crimsoned with our best blood; another, and it is blackened with the vilest treason. At one moment we have seemed to see a defined purpose; the next, and all is darkness and confusion. But at last the work is complete; all is revealed; all is part of one great scene, which all men understand, which all men may read and understand; nay, which all men *shall* read and understand.

It is the representation of a nation regenerated, of its rise above deadly theories, of its triumph over deadly practices, of its salvation from deadly systems.

But through all, from that first sad day to the day of joy unspeakable over liberty saved and nationality established, through the generalship and statesmanship, through the trials of blood and the trials of treason, wrought into all its texture, in and out through all its meshes, binding all together, brighter than all, stronger than all, receiving lustre from all victories, and casting lustre upon all defeats, runs a thread and strand of pure gold, the character of ABRAHAM LINCOLN.

A character this was, of pure intent, of high faith, of earnestness, of kindliness, manliness, godliness.

And now this great picture was finished, union, constitutionality, nationality, liberty everywhere triumphant; and by stalwart blows from the swords of our soldiers, the mighty fabric was detached, and as a separate history, displayed, to the joy of all who shall ever love truth and its triumphs.

We had hoped, oh, how fondly! we had expected, oh, how naturally! that this same golden thread of character, so pure, so strong, was to continue through time's next great fabric of four years, to enrich it, to beautify it, to purify it. Alas, it was not so to be. Amid the rejoicings at great national triumphs, this precious thread of existence is cut in a moment, and by the hand of an assassin. What was ABRAHAM LINCOLN, to all appearance lies to-day at the mouth of the tomb, a poor lump of chilled brain and withered muscle. The greatest series of national crimes ever known, begun four years ago by liberticide, are fitly ended by parricide.

The nation may well be sad. Never was ruler mourned as this ruler. It was given me, once, sir, to stand in the great capital of a great empire, when, in midst of a terrible war, the autocrat of seventy millions was suddenly stricken by death. But though nobles draped themselves in sables, and dames of high degree wore widow's weeds for half a year, it was not like this mourning, which drapes all in woe, and starts tears in the eyes of men whose pride is their stoicism.

And we stood by when, with roll of cannon, and chanting of choristers and prayers of prelates, the monarch was wrapped in his shroud of gold thread and laid in the tomb of his fathers; but that was not like this tender love of millions which deposits this martyr, oh, how lovingly, in his lowly grave.

And yet, though all this mourning, let us not yield for one moment to despair. Never have we had more to hope. It is a remark so common as now to be trite, that this history of four years shows everywhere traces of a divine guidance. You hear that assertion constantly from lips little given to moralizing or utterance of religious sentiments. But if this be true of the history of these events, it is even more true of the biography of this man called to take lead in these events.

Look at his birth, among the humblest; his cradle rocked and crooned over by those whom he was to deliver; look at his boyhood, passed with hardly any education, in a semi-barbarous society, but despite all that, he preserved every fine fibre of his nature; look at his youth when on those vast rivers of the west he became the companion and fellow workman of men whose disregard of all laws, human and divine, is a proverb, and from whose fellowship he emerges uncontaminated, and with a deep respect for law and order; look at him, as a young man, entering the noble profession of the law, avoiding that temptation which blights so much talent, the temptation to lead the life of the trickster and the pettifogger; look at him in full manhood, when all, far and near, spontaneously have prefixed to his name the title of "The Honest;" look at him in the highest of earthly seats, kindly, and great, and firm, while turbulence and intrigue seethe and surge around him.

Sir, our friend from the twenty-sixth district (Mr. FOLGER) has given us fitting words from him who "soared above the Aonian Mount." I, too, seemed to hear the words of liberty-loving MILTON. His prophetic sight seemed to have reached our late President, when he put words upon the lips of the chorus, viewing Samson Agonistes:

> O, how comely it is, and how reviving
> To the spirits of just men long oppressed,
> When God into the hands of their deliverer
> Puts strength to quell the mighty of the earth — the oppressor,
> The brute and boisterous force of violent men.
> *   *   *   *   *   *
> He all their ammunition
> And feats of war defeats,
> With plain, heroic magnitude of mind,
> And with celestial vigor armed.

Look, too, at this man, who, having done in four years what mightiest monarchs have failed to do in decades of years, with kindly expressions toward the vanquished, risking his popularity to shield them — he receives the blow of the assassin.

Can it be that the Omnipotent Hand which shaped these events so wonderfully, which prepared this man so wonderfully, has permitted his martyrdom without some wise purpose?

Our friend, the Senator from the twentieth district (Mr. ANDREWS), has presented a striking historical parallel. Let me for a moment direct you to another. When that great and good monarch, Henry the Fourth, of France, had led his nation through their terrible civil wars of the latter part of the sixteenth century, when peace was restored, when all mankind was loving and praising him who was before so reviled and hated, he was suddenly struck dead by the dagger of Ravaillac.

Deep, indeed, was the mourning. Patriots distrusted the Almighty. Anarchy set in. But soon, from the midst of the very classes who had fought so long and so bitterly—from the nobility and the clergy—came that great statesman, the Cardinal Duke of Richelieu, no longer kindly like his predecessor, but stern, filled with the idea that justice to individuals is the highest mercy to States. He it was who grasped rebellion and ended it. The assassin who deprived the nation of a ruler kind and gentle, gave the nation a ruler stern and inflexible.

Senators, let us here and now respond to the

appeal of our associate (Mr. FOLGER), who has called upon us to rise to higher phases of patriotic feeling. Over this, our great martyr, so much loved, so much revered, let hand grasp hand, let heart echo heart, let the vow arise that the nation shall be saved. Let us each to each, and all to all, give pledge that we will labor more and more to make this nation worthy of those two great forms which now tower above it, WASHINGTON and LINCOLN.

REMARKS OF MR. BAILEY.

The thoughts common to every American at this solemn moment, have already found such expression as human powers can give them. The resources of language have been exhausted. The pulpit and the press have spoken. We have listened here to-day to words of touching pathos. And while we have been so occupied, thousands of tongues all over the land have given utterance to the nation's sorrow.

And yet, the repetition does not tire us. So overwhelming is this calamity, that our minds reject all other subjects. It engrosses every faculty of our souls. It envelopes us with a dark pall that shuts out the events of earth, and almost the light of heaven. Like Rachel mourning for her children, we refuse to be comforted. The affairs of life, momentous as some of them are, cannot command our attention. The future, big with the fate of ourselves and of our children, is almost unheeded. We have received a blow which shocks and bewilders us. Had an earthquake opened its jaws and devoured the city of Washington and all it contained, we could hardly have been more appalled. "*President Lincoln has been assassinated!*" No living American can ever forget his sensations when that terrible message first reached him. He thought himself the victim of some horrible delusion, which yet could not be shaken off. He tried to believe it a dream, and struggled to awake from it. But turn where he would, listen to whom he would, his eyes and ears met only repetitions of the dreadful announcement. And yet he could not then realize the truth, and he can scarcely do so now. But alas! it was true. Abraham Lincoln was indeed no more. He had fallen a victim to the most cowardly and fiendish murder ever perpetrated on earth since the crucifixion. The world cannot find, in the vilest passions ever exhibited by mortal man, a sufficient incentive for this deed. We must search hell itself, and discover the unmixed, concentrated depravity of devils, to realize

"*The deep damnation of this taking off.*"

Oh! sir, what a great, unselfish, loving heart was laid in death by the hand of this infamous assassin! A heart that only yearned to bless and save; that would not willingly inflict suffering upon the meanest of mankind; that watched, and toiled, and prayed to bring back to peace and happiness, those who sought the nation's life; that could feel only pity and compassion, when vengeance at times swelled the souls of millions of our countrymen.

Not that Mr. LINCOLN was a mere sentimentalist. No man comprehended more clearly the necessity of force when treason was at work; and no man more firmly and steadfastly employed it. Again and again he summoned hundreds of thousands of his countrymen to the field; and while he gazed with sorrow upon the carnage which followed, he maintained an unalterable determination to fight out the war so long as armed resistance was made.

There were traits in the character of Mr. LINCOLN upon which the people of the United States, for all time to come, will love to dwell. Some of these have been pointed out by Senators who have preceded me. His honesty of purpose and devoted patriotism will never again be denied. If they ever have been, it was caused by the excitement of party strife, which, so far as Mr. LINCOLN is concerned, is gone forever. This great national affliction has brought us all together; to-day, at least, we are a band of brothers. We join hands over his grave, while heart throbs to heart.

Sir, I have studied Mr. LINCOLN for the last five years as I never did any other man, and it made me his enthusiastic admirer. If there were time, and this were a proper occasion, I should dearly love to speak of him as I feel. But I must not, here and now. I beg leave, in no spirit of controversy, however, to dissent from an opinion just expressed, that he was not, in the highest sense, a great man. I think he was, even intellectually, one of the greatest men ever born upon this continent. I know very well that this is not the general sentiment. His awkwardness of manner, simplicity of speech, quaintness of style, want of education and the polish it gives; in short, the contrast between his language and that of those whom the world recognizes as model men, have led to the common conclusion that he was not, in the highest sense, a great man. But I submit, that in the exhibition of pure intellectual power, he has had few equals, and no superiors in this country. I insist, that the ability to grasp a great subject which agitates the nation, and which bewilders and baffles the wisest, to strip it of all mystery, difficulty and extraneous matter, and place it before the people in so simple, clear and strong a light that the meanest capacity understands and appreciates it, is the very best test of intellectual superiority. And this ability Mr. LINCOLN possessed to a greater degree than any other man of his time. The world will yet do him justice in this respect.

But he is gone. His great work of putting down the rebellion was accomplished. That work required the highest and best qualities ever vouchsafed to man, and they were bestowed upon him. Intemperate zeal and wild impetuosity could not disturb him. Sophistry could not deceive him. The clamors of friends and the threats of foes alike failed to move him. Knowing that the responsibility rested upon himself, he relied only upon God and the conclusions of his own judgment. Acknowledging his dependence upon the people, and never acting without their sanction, he yet gave direction to popular opinion, and led it to the desired conclusions. He had finished his work, although ready, God willing, to undertake the further task of quieting the land so long rent by civil war. He had secured the respect and confidence, if not the love, of all his loyal countrymen. Every man felt that the final adjustment of our difficulties was safe in his hands. But he has been taken from us. We now see that our deliverance is not to come from man, but from the Almighty Ruler of the Universe. And holding fast to the faith which He has taught us, we confidently believe, and unhesitatingly say, that this country will still live.

The assassin who committed this foul murder undoubtedly expected to aid the cause of treason, but he only hastened its extermination. Whatever may have been the feelings of some of us in the past, to-day there is not a man at the North who would not smother the last spark of the infernal spirit which prompts such deeds. These rebels have struck down, in President LINCOLN, their wisest, truest and most powerful friend. Such is the short-sightedness of crime. The Redeemer of the world was crucified and slain by the very men he yearned to save.

It may be, that it was necessary to permit this exhibition of the real character of the rebellion. Its wantonness and general wickedness had already been seen, but the utter barbarism and savageness which underlies it, was, perhaps, not entirely comprehended. Notwithstanding its championship of slavery, its attempt to destroy free government from off the earth, its atrocious treatment of prisoners, still, the innate satanic spirit which inspired it was not realized. Perhaps it was necessary that this spirit should be concentrated into a single act of sufficient atrocity to shock the world. It was thus seen in this murder. Hereafter, when mankind seek to illustrate the lowest depths to which human depravity can sink, they will point to the assassination of President LINCOLN.

REMARKS OF MR. LOW.

Mr. PRESIDENT: We have lived to see the darkest day in American history—the memory of which appals the stoutest heart and fills our land with wailing and lamentation. The curtain has now arisen upon the last act of the bloody drama in which we are the actors; and men and nations stand aghast in bewilderment and horror. A wicked and fiendish rebellion—born in treason and baptized in blood—has culminated in murder and assassination. The same fell spirit which fired upon our country's flag, which drove the Southern Unionists with baying blood-hounds to dens and caverns; which tortured with slow and dreadful death the Union soldiers in Southern dungeons, and butchered captive prisoners upon the field of war—has now struck down the friend of liberty, the champion of the oppressed.

Our loved and trusted Chieftain is no more—an American President, great and good and honored throughout the land, is stricken down by the hand of violence in the heyday of his usefulness and in the brilliant dawning of his triumphs.

We have in this dread struggle offered up our brightest jewels upon the altar of our country. We have given our fair-haired boys to die in rebel dungeons. Our bravest and our best, have gone down upon the gory battle-field—and now the costliest sacrifice of all—the "foremost man" in all the world is, too, a victim to the demon spirit which has filled our land with orphans and crimsoned its soil with blood.

It is yet too early to estimate our loss or form a just conception of the character of the dead. Since the day when Egypt's trembling bondmen followed their deliverer from the land of slavery, there has lived no mortal man whose name the coming millions will shout so gladly as that of Liberty's great martyr, for whom we mourn.

Other men have died for truth, and fallen in the cause of right; other rulers have battled well for freedom and marshaled armies against the tyrants of the world; but it was reserved for this champion of human liberty to have fought the decisive battle for "the inalienable rights of man," and to have sanctified the victory by his immolation upon its shrine.

The oppressed have lost a benefactor; the bondmen their deliverer, and our country its second father. History will assign no second place to the name of ABRAHAM LINCOLN. High up upon its scroll, above the mighty ones and conquerors of the earth, will his be written, a watchword for the slave, a rallying cry for freemen, the terror of the tyrant, the joy of the oppressed; NAPOLEON will be forgotten; CÆSAR will cease to be remembered; CROMWELL will be known no more; but far down through the vista of coming centuries, till the sands of time shall cease to run, will be hailed with glad acclaim the memory of our martyred hero, for whom the people weep, and the nations mourn.

But our country must not die, our faith in God must not be shaken. The same kind Providence which led our way through storms and darkness, and guided our armies through fire and blood, will not desert us now.

Tyrant's thrones will crumble to the dust, and trembling despotisms will be remembered with the hated things that were; but the deep foundations of our nation's liberties, consecrated by her children's blood, are destined to endure while nations live. To us has been reserved the trial which is to test the power of Liberty, the manhood of our race; and though bloody is the pathway and terrible the ordeal, the awful responsibility is still upon us and must be met, a mighty destiny still wills us onward and bids us faint and falter not. "Out of danger must safety come." It is trial that gives us strength, suffering that gives us fortitude, conflict that lends us courage, blood that consecrates the cause of truth, and patriot martyrdom that gives it life eternal.

With blinded Justice for our chart and compass, with faith in God and love to man to guide our hearts, let us go calmly forward and finish the great work that God has destined for us.

REMARKS OF MR. WILLIAMS.

Mr. PRESIDENT: I desire to mingle my sad feelings in the expressions of regret which this occasion calls forth. A great and a good man has fallen; and it always seems to me that the good die first. Bad men live, but the good fall in the midst of their labors. A great and good man, a nation's President, has suddenly been struck down by the hand of an assassin. This rebellion, this unholy warfare, costing as much as it has in the blood, the heroic devotion, of loyal and patriotic men; men dying on the battlefield; men dying in hospitals; men who, in their last breath, have cheered the country's flag, and died with a blessing on their lips for the land they loved so well; men dying in prisons, starved by more than hellish malignity; the untold suffering, the deprivation, both at home and in the army, which this rebellion has cost—the whole series of horrors is outstripped and overshadowed by the intelligence that our loved President lies dead, by the hand of an assassin.

Although he did not live to fill out the measure of his country's glory, yet no name will be grander in history than that of ABRAHAM LINCOLN—none truer, none better. Who with so pure a heart, who with so single a purpose, who with so inflexible a will has conducted this war as ABRAHAM LINCOLN? Of those who have given themselves for the benefit of mankind, of those who have given their time and their lives for the elevation of their race, history will record no name that has accomplished more than he. It seems as though, if the world could be governed by such men for a few generations, freedom would be advanced and the welfare of the masses promoted to a degree never before known.

I have said the brave and good die first. Witness BRODERICK, almost a founder of an empire on our western shores, killed by cold blooded assassination, although according to the supposed and miscalled laws of honor. President TAYLOR, cut off in the midst of his usefulness, and when a nation were looking to him to conduct them through a critical time. President HARRISON, who, in the entrance of his great public career, succumbed to the power of the fell destroyer. So men in the career of their usefulness seem cut down. The evil live.

Yet one thing must be remarked, that, although when such men fall, we, their countrymen, look round to see who shall lead us now, in whom we shall trust our hopes and our destinies; yet we always find that an overruling Providence leads us on. God still protects and preserves the nation. Although men fall, principles live. May we not trust that He will lead us through the evil times which we have fallen upon, through our affliction; and although our leader, cut down like Moses, not being permitted to enjoy with his people the fruition of his labors, still the nation and the people, and the cause of truth and righteousness, will be preserved and upheld by an overruling Providence.

I have not forgotten that a favored son of New

York, an honored, a loved citizen of one of the counties which I represent, has lain at the point of death by the hand of an assassin. His record, one of the proudest that the history of our country presents, yet pales before his social virtues. He exists in the love of the people of this State, and no name will stand higher when the history of this rebellion is written—nay, even now, in the written history of this crisis—than his.

But, Mr. President, it is not for me to pronounce their eulogy. History will pronounce it—the untold millions of this and future ages will bear that history in their hearts, where forever will live the names united of ABRAHAM LINCOLN and WILLIAM H. SEWARD.

And the son of the Secretary of State, standing high in the estimation of the public for his worth, his amiability and his social qualities, was nearly stricken to death by the hand of the same assassin, in his efforts to protect and save the life of his father.

From out of this dread deed let us pluck security to the future. Turn we to the living. Standing here over the grave of LINCOLN, dropping tears to his ashes, let us renew our allegiance to the cause of liberty. It is right that from us, on this day, should go forth to the people whom we represent, the words of courage and encouragement. Be true to your country in this her hour of trial. Stand fast by the powers that be. Sustain and strengthen the government of the people. It is our only salvation, under the mercy and the guidance of a good God. Let us be true to the work which Providence has given us to perform, to help work out the great destinies of this nation.

No cause existed for the death of our chief. Upon the very day when this traitor's hand took his life, he meditated nothing but kindness and forgiveness to our enemies.

To think that, in this hour of his generosity, in triumph, while his great kind heart was so full of sympathy and kindness for the South, that he should be struck down by the assassin's bullet, while he never entertained an unkind thought towards any one, it is enough to make the nation weep. And yet, the cause is safe for which martyrs die. It is the record of all time, that the death of martyrs makes the cause secure. It is as much the case as that the death of traitors is the true cement of liberty.

Secession assassins have drowned the voice of mercy in behalf of secession leaders, in the universal public voice for justice, and for the protection of the nation in its appointed rulers.

For his own personal fame, no fitter time, perhaps, could have happened for his death than now. He dies at a time when the country is almost restored to peace through his direction of public affairs—when a race enslaved for years, by his agency becomes free. There needed only this manner of his death to canonize him in the hearts of the people. His name will live as a martyr to liberty, to the freedom and advancement of the whole race.

> Rest, LINCOLN, rest!
> Rest in thy laureled tomb!
> Laureled by the freedom of a race!
> Thy memory shall live through all earth's years;
> And thy name shall excite the despots' fears,
> While o'er thee shall fall a nation's tears.

But while we contemplate the dead body of our chief, let us not forget the duties of the hour. It is fitting that we here renew our pledge to liberty. It is fitting that, standing here, over the remains of our honored dead, we pledge ourselves anew to the cause of our bleeding country, till humanity shall be regenerated in the advancing steps of freedom, and upon this land's domain no slave shall breathe.

From out of this cloud of gloom and despondency let us still look with hope to the future. Our domestic tranquility is still undisturbed by this dread event. The nation's heart never beat truer to the nation's cause. ANDREW JOHNSON, upon whom the mantle of our leader has fallen, is a true and tried statesman, a firm and devoted patriot, and worthy of our fullest confidence. To him we would say, " Guide thou the ship of state to the desired haven of universal freedom and emancipation, to which it is now directed."

> From out the dusk of far receding centuries
> One clear prophetic voice of warning calls;
> 'Tis this, that in the hour of trust and trial,
> He who falters, falls!
> Oh! hearken to it, thou to-day, who holdest
> In thy hand a nation's wavering fate,
> And be thou truest of the true, and boldest
> Of the bold! We wait—
> We wait, thy people, patient but expectant;
> And the far nations, tip-toe, stand agape,
> While thou dost solve the problem of the present,
> And giv'st the future certainty and shape!

REMARKS OF MR. HAVENS.

Mr. PRESIDENT: There are times when the very effort to express the thoughts and feelings of our hearts but demonstrate the utter inadequacy of language to give them utterance.

The throbbing heart struggles in vain to relieve itself from its pangs of woe and swelling grief by sympathetic communication with the outer world.

There are times in our pilgrimage on earth, when poor finite vision can discover naught but darkness and desolation in the decrees of Him who doeth all things well—when an impenetrable gloom seems to shut out every bright and cheering prospect in the future, and in spite of our faith in God, the heart sinks in overwhelming anguish and despair under his chastening rod.

Often have such times overtaken us in the rapid succession of great events during the last four years in our beloved country.

From the boundless exultation of joy at the triumph of our arms over the enemies of our country, the nation is suddenly thrown into tears of anguish and grief at the loss of him whom we have the second time chosen to lead us through our remaining conflicts and trials, and in whose wisdom, firmness and moderation were centered our brightest hopes and anticipations of the future.

The nation is bereaved of its father—its guardian —its protector—and we are to-day all weeping, inconsolable orphans.

Having led us through nearly all our difficulties, having brought us under the divine blessing to the banks of deliverance from the bloody conflicts of civil war, and gained sight of the bright hill tops of that land of rest, of freedom and universal liberty which we all hoped soon to reach, he is stricken down by the hand of the assassin, and his own careworn, weary spirit has found its rest in that celestial world—that holier land where war, bloodshed and civil strife are never known.

Mr. President, I cannot say more. I have no heart to talk, when words are so feeble for their use in bearing the messages of the heart.

Let us yield an humble resignation to this afflicting dispensation of an all-wise and merciful Providence. Let us still cherish hope that our beloved country will survive all its losses and afflictions, and that the blood of our noble President shall cement us in a more perfect Union, and inspire our hearts with a firmer and more constant devotion to the support of those principles of free government for which we have contended, and stimulate us to renewed efforts to bring our country out of its turmoil and strife, to an honorable and abiding peace, and place it upon that highway of prosperity among the nations of earth, to accomplish which our President labored with unremitting and successful effort up to the moment when the sacrifice of his life sent pain and anguish to all our hearts.

REMARKS OF MR. STRONG.

Ninety years ago this day, in the streets of Lexington, the sacrifice of patriot life began for the establishment of this nation.

Four years ago this day, in the streets of Baltimore, the blood of our soldiers was shed while on their way to the protection of our national life.

To-day we meet in solemn sadness to mourn a greater calamity. Another martyr has been sacrificed upon the altar of our country. The blood of our murdered President stains the streets of our national capital, and cries aloud for *justice*. Eighteen hundred years ago, our spiritual salvation was made possible by the death of the Saviour. HIS death did for the world what no act of his life could have accomplished. The death of ABRAHAM LINCOLN renders it not only possible, but has already cemented all loyal hearts upon one common purpose, and hereafter the spirit of *Mercy* will be attended with a sterner and more retributive JUSTICE. We mourn, but not without hope.

Mr. COLE offered the following resolution:

Whereas, It is represented that the remains of the deceased President, ABRAHAM LINCOLN, will pass through the principal cities on the line of the Central railroad, and that a brief stop will be made in this city; therefore,

Resolved (if the Assembly concur), That a committee consisting of three from the Senate and five from the Assembly, be appointed to meet those having the remains of the deceased in charge, at the city of New York, and accompany them through the State; and that the Lieutenant-Governor be added to said joint committee as the chairman thereof.

By unanimous consent the rule was suspended, when,

The President put the question whether the Senate would agree to said resolution, and it was decided in the affirmative.

Ordered, That the Clerk deliver said resolution to the Assembly, with a message requesting their concurrence therein.

Friday, April 21.

The Assembly returned the resolution, with a message that they have passed the same, with the following amendment:

Insert after the word " appointed " the following: " To act in concert with the Governor of the State and the Commander of this Division, deputed by the War Department for that purpose, and with the municipal authorities of Albany in perfecting arrangements for the reception of the body of the deceased President at the Capital of the State, and,"

The President put the question whether the Senate would agree to concur in said amendment, and it was decided in the affirmative.

Ordered, That the Clerk return said resolution to the Assembly, with a message that the Senate have concurred in their amendment.

Hon. THOMAS G. ALVORD, Lieutenant-Governor, and Messrs. COLE, LAIMBEER and CHRISTIE were announced as such committee on behalf of the Senate, and Messrs. WOOD, VAN BUREN, COLLINS, BURDITT and INGRAHAM, on behalf of the Assembly.

The Senate took a recess.

Printed in Poland
by Amazon Fulfillment
Poland Sp. z o.o., Wrocław

68426411R00070